Listening for God

LISTENING *for* GOD

Marilyn Hontz

Tyndale House Publishers, Inc.
Wheaton, Illinois

Library of Congress Cataloging-in-Publication Data

Hontz, Marilyn.
    Listening for God : how an ordinary person can learn to hear God speak / Marilyn Hontz.
        p. cm.
Includes bibliographical references.
    ISBN 0-8423-8539-8 (sc)
    1. Word of God (Theology) 2. Revelation. 3. Listening—Religious aspects—Christianity. I. Title.
BT180.W67H66 2004
231.7—dc22   2003022001

Printed in the United States of America

08 07 06 05 04
6   5   4   3   2   1

Dedicated to
Marion Uzon Miller:
the one who first prayed for me and modeled
listening for God—
my mother.

My heart has heard you say,
"Come and talk with me."
And my heart responds,
"Lord, I am coming."
Psalm 27:8, NLT

CONTENTS

Introduction   xi

PART 1: RECOGNIZING GOD'S VOICE WHILE READING SCRIPTURE
Chapter 1: Words to Live By   3
Chapter 2: God in the Ordinary   13
Chapter 3: Finding God in His Word   25

PART 2: RECOGNIZING GOD'S VOICE WHILE PRAYING
Chapter 4: "Lord, Teach Me to Pray"   41
Chapter 5: Adventures in Listening Prayer   51
Chapter 6: Finding God in Prayer   63
Chapter 7: Bringing Prayer out of the Closet   77
Chapter 8: When Praying Isn't Easy   89
Chapter 9: Capturing the Spirit of Prayer:
             Slinky the Caterpillar   113

PART 3: RECOGNIZING GOD'S VOICE WHILE LISTENING
Chapter 10: Stopping to Listen   123
Chapter 11: Does God Speak to His Children?   139
Chapter 12: How Does God Speak to His Children?   151
Chapter 13: Reaping the Rewards of Listening   171

Appendix A: Bible Study Tools   191
Appendix B: A Prayer Test   195
Appendix C: T.A.W.G. (Time Alone with God)   197
Endnotes   205

In Gratitude

*M*y gratitude extends to many people, some who are well-known and others who are obscure to the world but known to the Lord and to me.

- Dr. James and Shirley Dobson, who encouraged me to write and not "hide my light under a bushel."
- Kathleen Hart, my mentor who prays daily and reminds me often that I am always playing to an "audience of One." This friend is a true intercessor.
- Danae Dobson, who sent frequent e-mails and forwards to cheer me on.
- Janis Long Harris, editors Kim Miller and Karin Buursma, and the rest of the Tyndale team, who extended a gracious invitation to me to write.
- The 139 "Lydia Ladies" and a team of 99 men who are a part of my husband's prayer support team. These people prayed me through the writing process.

- Jack and Mary DeWitt, Judy Hupe, Carole Bos, Doc and Joyce Heatherly, Pam Holmes, Heidi Harlow, and Loie Grotler—all encouragers who called, e-mailed, wrote letters, and prayed about this book from the beginning to the end.
- My precious family, whom I am crazy about. My husband, Paul, who since we first met has remained an answer to my prayers. He also encouraged me with this book and told me to "let other stuff go and write." (I took that to mean housework.)
- Christy, Holly, Mandy, Abby, and Paul Matthew, who allowed me to write about them and each day asked, "How's the book going, Mom?" Special thanks to Christy and Mandy who spent many hours reading the manuscript and making suggestions; I could not have written without them. And a big thank-you to Paul Matthew who, with his computer expertise, rescued me many times.
- My godly in-laws, Paul and Doris Jane Hontz, who have loved and encouraged me throughout this project as well.
- And to the Lord Jesus, who gave me this opportunity to write about him in the first place. I am deeply grateful.

"Now glory be to God, who by his mighty power at work within us is able to do far more than we would ever dare to ask or even dream of—infinitely beyond our highest prayers, desires, thoughts, or hopes." (Ephesians 3:20, TLB)

Introduction

September 21, 1966. As the fighting heated up in my brother's Marine unit in Vietnam, our family was facing a battle of another kind. My mother had just returned from a nearly two-month stay at UCLA Medical Center. I had missed her terribly and was relieved to have her home.

My older sister, Joyce, called me into the den to see our mother. "Mother is asking for you, Marilyn," she said. "Try not to cry, honey," she added kindly as she softly closed the door behind me.

I sat down next to my mother, who lay on a pullout sofa bed. With the exception of Buttons, our Chihuahua, who guarded her with fierce loyalty, our small den resembled a sterile hospital room. A green oxygen tank stood sentry beside her bed. I could hear hushed conversations outside the door.

My mother looked pale and thin. Her high cheekbones were even more pronounced because of her weight loss. She seemed so fragile that I was almost afraid to touch her. Her dark brown eyes searched mine and she smiled. She gently reached for my hand, pulled me close, and just held me for a few minutes.

"Honey, I need to share something with you," Mother finally said. "My disease is not going to heal." She did not use the word *cancer,* but I knew. Her breast cancer had spread. I couldn't believe it! I had been begging God to heal her. Only a few days before I had told the Lord that I had all the faith in the world that he would heal her. I truly believed he would.

I had reminded God that he needed my mother on earth! *After all,* I had told him, *she teaches Bible studies at two churches. She gives devotions at my public school's PTO meetings.* (Quite a privilege, considering that all the other committee members were Jewish. They loved my mother!) *She is a great pastor's wife, plus you know that she is very good at introducing people to you. Most importantly,* I *need her here on earth! Children are not supposed to lose their mother when they are fourteen,* I had pleaded.

Now I was faced with the stark reality that God was not answering my prayers the way I had expected. I threw myself on my mother, sobbing and clinging to her as if I were in a tug-of-war with death itself. She let me grieve as she held me.

"Why hasn't God answered your prayers?" I demanded. "He usually does."

She responded with an honest, simple answer: "Honey, I really don't know. I do know that the Lord has assured me that you will be okay."

I remember thinking, *Oh, that's easy for you to say; you are going away, and I am staying here.*

Frankly, I was afraid to lose her. My brother, Cliff, the Marine, was eight years older than I. (The Red Cross had located him in battle and allowed him to come home to say good-bye to our mother.) My sister, Joyce, was twenty years older and lived with her family two hours away. My dad was a busy pastor, but we were not emotionally close. My mother was the nurturing parent—my teacher, my mentor, and my friend. My life revolved around her and *her* relationship with God.

We talked a bit more about who was going to take care of me after she died. She began struggling for air in spite of the respirator and was obviously in great pain. My family decided she needed to return to the hospital. We loaded her into our station wagon and rode with her back to the medical center. After a nurse quickly got her ready for bed, I leaned down, kissed her good night, and told her I loved her. As I was leaving her room, I said, "I'm not going to school tomorrow, so I will see you in the morning."

She smiled and said, "Okay." Those were our last words. She died early the next morning. I felt abandoned by my mother, and my strongest connection to God died with her.

LIVING LEGACY

My mother was the first person who modeled prayer and listening to God for me. She prayed with me before I left for school each day. She prayed with people over the phone. Often I would see her talking with someone one moment and then praying with that person the next.

I knew the Bible was the most important book to her. She always kept memory verses, printed on cards, in her purse. Each Saturday morning we sat in our kitchen as she discipled me from a Bible workbook for kids. I loved licking the Bible picture stamps and placing them in the book. I looked forward to these special one-on-one times with my mom. It was during those Saturday sessions that I came to realize my mother considered God her dearest friend.

When I was twelve, I told my mother I didn't have any friends. We talked about it, and then she prayed with me that the Lord would bring a friend into my life. After we prayed, she said she had an idea. She suggested that the next day I look around the lunchroom for another girl who was eating lunch alone and ask if I could join her. That is how I met my friend Julie. Not long after we met, I invited Julie over to our house. Before the end of her first visit, my mother had led her to know Jesus in a personal way. My mother wasn't pushy; it was just second nature for her to acquaint people with her dearest Friend.

Only days before she died, I asked her if I could read to her from the Bible. She said, "Read the first chapter of Colossians from the *Living Letters* version." As I began to read to her, I noticed that she was quoting from memory, word for word, the entire chapter! She lived in what I call a "vibrant communication" with her heavenly Father. Prayer was simply her way of talking with God about *everything*.

I wanted the kind of relationship with God that my mother had. Instead, I felt like I was hanging on to her spiritual apron strings and following behind her. What was her secret of being so close to Jesus?

A short time after my mother's death, my sister, Joyce, began sorting my mother's things. She discovered a cupboard full of prayer journals and notebooks. I had not seen them before, and it was powerful to look through the pages and see Mother's familiar handwriting. I flipped through one journal and saw my name, the date, and details on how she was praying for me at that specific time.

One of those notebooks contained a story about a missionary doctor. My sister had discovered its significance to our mother when she came home for a visit during Mother's illness. Quietly entering Mother's bedroom when she arrived, Joyce thought Mother was asleep until she noticed her smiling. When she asked what had happened, Mother said, "Oh, Joyce honey, I've had the most wonderful experience."

She told Joyce that she was reading a book about Dr. Paul

Carlson, a medical missionary to the Democratic Republic of Congo (once Zaire) in the 1960s. She'd just been reading about how he had been running toward the safety of a stone wall by the mission compound when Congolese rebels had shot him to death. The area was liberated only fifteen minutes later—but of course that was fifteen minutes too late for him.

Mother said that when she'd come to that part of Dr. Carlson's story, she had put the book down, furious at God for allowing this dedicated doctor to die.

After all, she had mentally shouted at God, *he was only in his thirties. He was a doctor, hard at work to heal people and further your cause. Why did you do that to him? Why did you cut him down in the prime of his life and ministry? What mean joke were you playing on him? You let him go to Africa and serve you, and then you allow him to be shot just as he was about to reach the safety of the stone wall?*

"Of course," said Mother, "what I was really downright mad about was why God allowed *me* to have such a ministry, one that was so blessed by his touch, when he was planning on taking me. Why now?" It was the first time Joyce had heard her admit that she was terminally ill. The moment tore Joyce apart and she began to weep.

"Don't cry, honey," Mother said. "Do you know how the Lord answered my questions about Dr. Carlson?"

"No, how?" Joyce asked. (She was thinking, *I should have known he'd answer her!*)

"Well, the Lord seemed to be saying, 'Marion, you think Dr. Carlson was busy and effective for me and my work there in the Congo? Oh, Marion, you should see him now!'" Mother's eyes glistened with tears as she continued, "'Marion, my dear child, you think you're busy there in Reseda, California? Just wait till you get here!'"[1]

[1]Joyce Landorf Heatherley, *Mourning Song* (Grand Rapids, Mich.: Fleming H. Revell, 1994), 84–85.

My mother sensed the Lord speaking to her about her circumstances through the story of Dr. Carlson. She experienced an abiding peace as God spoke to her heart.

When Joyce told me about their conversation, I realized that my mother had struggled with many of the same questions that I had. At some point in her battle against breast cancer, she knew her earthly life would be cut short. She was teaching Bible studies, she was helping women come to know God, and she still had me, a young teenager, at home. Surely God's timing was off! It just didn't make sense.

Yet, she found out that God could handle her anger with him, and she experienced an abiding peace that enabled her to relinquish me completely into her loving heavenly Father's arms.

As I sat next to her in the den the night before she died, I remember her telling me: "Marilyn, while I will not be able to meet your husband or hold your babies in my arms, I am 'holding' them in prayer. I have been praying for your future husband and your future children."

She was planting seeds of prayer deeply in the soil of my heart—seeds that would sprout years later. I would learn that although human life is limited, our prayers have no boundaries. They can stretch out over generations. "Prayers are deathless," said E. M. Bounds. "Prayers outlive the lives of those who uttered them; outlive a generation, outlive an age, outlive a world."[2] Today I believe my husband and children still reap the effects of her mighty, prevailing prayers.

Although I didn't fully understand it then, I had found my mother's secret! She talked everything over with the Lord, taking time to listen for his response. Though God didn't speak audibly to her, she received a quiet inner impression from the Holy Spirit that gave her peace. He flooded her with his *partici-*

[2]Leonard Ravenhill, comp., *A Treasury of Prayer* (Minneapolis, Minn.: Bethany House Publishers, 1961), 61.

pating presence. Even when she faced her own death, she was filled with an incredible sense of calm because she recognized her heavenly Father's voice and he had given her his perspective on eternity.

AN ADVENTURE IN LISTENING

What about you? Do you long to approach God as you would a dear friend? Is it truly possible for you to hear God speak today? You can learn to recognize God's voice, if you listen! You don't need to be a super-religious person to hear from God. All you need is a hunger for him and a listening ear.

I have found what many have discovered: God speaks to each of us through his Holy Word, and he communicates with us as we pray. He whispers to us through his Holy Spirit in the quietness of our hearts. He does this because he wants us to be in an intimate relationship with him—a relationship he desired before we were even created. A. W. Tozer said, "[God] waits to be wanted. Too bad that with many of us He waits so long, so very long, in vain."[3] He waits for *you* to want him!

If God wants to open his heart to us, why is it so difficult to hear his voice? How do we respond when we feel like God is ignoring our pleas, as I felt while watching my mother's life slip away?

The rest of this book explores my adventures in learning to hear God speak through the Word and prayer as I stilled myself and listened for his voice. My journey has not always been a smooth, easy one, and my aim is not to tell you *how* to build your devotional life. Rather, I hope the Scriptures and my personal experiences will create in you a deep hunger to spend time in God's presence and learn to recognize his voice.

Listening is a lot like waiting. When we're in the midst of either, we often feel like we are wasting time. Paradoxically, some of God's greatest gifts come in the still hours we spend in

[3]A. W. Tozer, *The Pursuit of God* (Camp Hill, Penn.: Christian Publications, Inc., 1993), 17.

his presence. When we really learn to hear God's voice, we allow him to share his plans with us and actually involve us in his work! We never know what truth God will show us or how he will impact others through us, but one thing is sure: Life becomes an adventure.

God is always listening to you. He invites you to listen to him as well. "Be still, and know that I am God," he says to you (Psalm 46:10). Listen. . . .

Recognizing God's Voice While Reading Scripture

Words to Live By

*B*y age thirty, I seemed to have put the pain of my mother's death behind me. I had married Paul, a caring man, when I was twenty. Now, ten years into our marriage, he was pastoring a growing church. I was busy launching a women's ministries program, playing the piano during worship services, teaching Bible studies, and housing guests. My husband and I were also rearing three daughters, aged six and under.

While my life may have appeared perfect on the outside, I was miserable inside. After my mother's death, I had desperately wanted to connect with my dad as I had with my mother. I had longed for him to put his arms around me and tell me that he loved me. I had tried to please my dad and live up to his expectations, but I never quite felt good enough and sensed I was a burden to him. While I believe that deep down he loved me, it seemed as if we were miles apart emotionally. I kept hoping that my dad would change, but he never did.

Seeds of bitterness that had been planted during my teen years were growing and choking the life out of me. I likened my bitterness to a pair of handcuffs. My hand was in one cuff and my dad's hand was in the other, and I ended up mentally dragging him with me wherever I went each day. But dwelling on and rehearsing the hurts he had caused kept me in bondage. The old saying "Bitterness is like acid; it only eats up the container that holds it" is true. I was being eaten alive.

DRAWN TO THE BOOK

A step toward change came in a surprising way. That summer I received my first invitation to speak at a conference. I was asked to speak on the topic "Daily Devotions" at a youth convention in Urbana, Illinois, during the upcoming Christmas break. When I first received the invitation, I groaned inwardly. First of all, the thought of speaking to two thousand teens was frightening; I had never enjoyed public speaking. Second, and more important, how could I teach something I did not do myself? Others probably assumed I read my Bible daily. After all, I loved God, I had been raised in a pastor's home, and I was a pastor's wife.

Actually, although I knew the importance of reading the Bible, I had thought I could get by just reading it once in a while or on Sundays. I justified this by assuring myself that the Lord understood how busy I was with church and family matters. I just had too much to do to have a regular quiet time.

God was getting my *leftover* time, if even that. I couldn't remember the last time I had given him my *best* time. As I prayed about speaking to those teens, I knew I could only accept that speaking invitation if I got into the Word myself. Bothered by my lack of discipline and pressed by the conference organizers to give them an answer, I sought out Joy, another pastor's wife.

"Do you have devotions every day?" I asked her. She said,

"Yes, I do. I've been doing it consistently for the past five years."

I was amazed! Joy had four young children, yet she had read her Bible every day for the past five years. "How do you do it, and how do I get started?" I asked with much skepticism. Her answer dramatically changed the way I read Scripture.

READ UNTIL GOD SPEAKS TO YOU

"Start today!" she challenged. "Ask God to speak to you from his Word, and read until he shows you an insight, promise, correction, or encouragement." So that was it. *Read the Word of God until the Lord speaks to you.*

I whined that I didn't think I had the discipline to do this every day. Joy reminded me that doing something for twenty-one days makes it become a habit. I was still skeptical. "Marilyn," Joy said, "simply read the Word until God speaks to you. You may read only one paragraph, but if you sense your heavenly Father stopping you, then pause and see what God wants to do with that passage in your life for that day."

Since the Word of God contains powerful truths, it will take considerable time to digest it, she said. Joy encouraged me to keep a notebook and write down the verse that I sensed God speaking to me about.

As I considered Joy's advice, I realized that deep inside I was tired of my excuses for not being in the Word on a daily basis. I wanted to do something about it. I wasn't merely feeling a guilt trip brought on by the upcoming speaking engagement; I was being convicted by the Holy Spirit. For the first time, I was hungry for the Bread of Life.

I began to read the Word at night before I went to bed. I started at the beginning of the Bible and read until I sensed the Holy Spirit wanted me to catch something. Sometimes I read only a few verses before I stopped. Sometimes I read a couple of chapters, but there was always a truth for me to learn. I also read some psalms each day, as they comforted me in my continued inward struggle over the lack of connection with my dad.

I read with an expectation that God would, indeed, speak to my heart. Most nights a word, verse, or phrase seemed to lift off the page at me. I was amazed at how many verses just "happened" to fit with my experiences that day.

During this time before the conference, I read Psalm 119. Verses 16 and 18 caught my attention: "I delight in your decrees; I will not neglect your word" (v. 16). "Open my eyes that I may see wonderful things in your law" (v. 18).

Lord Jesus, I prayed, *please help me not to neglect your Word any longer. Open my eyes to see the wonderful things you want to teach me. Help me to be disciplined in this. It is important to you and it is essential for me. Help me see that I cannot live one day without your Living Word.* The Lord did, in fact, help me to begin hungering for his Word.

Five months later, I stood before those two thousand teens and shared how a thirty-year-old woman had finally gotten into the Word. I urged them not to wait so long. After the session, many teens (and adults) told me that they too struggled to read the Bible daily. Some confessed that while they were eager to read (and reread) love letters from their boyfriend or girlfriend, they lacked the same desire to read the Bible—God's "love letter" to them.

DRAWING ON THE BOOK

The energy and joy I felt after speaking at Urbana quickly turned into anxiety when I returned home to discover that some conflicts within our church were about to boil over. A group of about thirty from our fellowship desired to go in a different direction from what the church leadership had planned. Every day during this trying time, I poured out my heart to God. Did the Word of God have answers for this difficult situation? I wondered.

I soon had my answer, as the psalms I read came alive and seemed to have been written just for me. The psalm writers addressed the very issues I was experiencing—betrayal, unfair treatment, and the desire to escape to a far-off place. Psalm 55:6-8 in particular spoke powerfully to me: "Oh, that I had the wings of a dove! I would fly away and be at rest—I would flee far away and stay in the desert; I would hurry to my place of shelter, far from the tempest and storm."

> *I lie in the dust, completely discouraged; revive me by your word.*
>
> **Psalm 119:25, NLT**

I became desperate for God and searched my Bible each night for a thread of hope. I wanted to leave our congregation, but Paul did not feel released by the Lord to do so. Because this difficult situation lasted a few years, I was forced to stay in the Word. Later I saw how the Lord used the pain of those experiences to shape me solely by his Word. Would I seek human help, or would I go to the Lord first?

As the dissension persisted, I wrote over and over in my journal, "Father, how long is this going to go on?" Yet I ended every page with a promise from Scripture that the Lord would work out his purposes.

My journal entry for December 28, 1983, reads, "Dear Father, help me to trust you during these next few months. We have received a 'prophecy' from a disgruntled person in the congregation who says that 'God is going to close the doors of Central Wesleyan Church at the close of December 1983.' Is this true?" It continues, "I wonder what 1984 holds? Father, the situation we are going through is so desperate . . . these are rough days, please give us clear direction. I feel so frightened. Do you want us to leave Central? I sometimes get the feeling we should leave. Either help us overcome or let us go—whatever you want." My journal entry for that day concluded with Ephesians 3:20 (TLB): "Now glory be to God who by his mighty power at work within us is able to do far more than we would ever dare to ask or even dream of—infinitely beyond our highest prayers, desires, thoughts, or hopes."

In spite of that bright promise, it didn't seem possible that God could do *anything* through us, let alone do "far more than we would ever dare to ask." It was hard to trust him because of all the hurt we were experiencing.

December of 1983 came and went and the church doors were still open. However, by May 1984 discouragement and depression lay heavy on our hearts. My journal reveals that "we have learned that our 'friends' have turned against us. This is a hard rejection to take, Father. I know that you understand how we feel."

Thirty people had left to form a new church. I was tired of seeing my husband hurt. "Honey," I said one evening when he returned very late from a board meeting, "I will gladly pack our bags if you will just give me the okay." Paul still did not feel at peace about leaving.

WORDS FROM ANOTHER

In the midst of my despair, I learned that sometimes God enables others to comfort us through his Word. One afternoon, as I was kneeling beside my bed praying about the heavy cloud of discouragement I was under, the phone rang. My father-in-law had been praying for us and was calling to share a verse he had just read. "I believe this verse is for you and Paul. Listen: 'But the God of all grace, who has called you to His eternal glory in Christ, will, after you have *suffered awhile*, Himself *equip, stabilize, strengthen, and firmly establish you*' (1 Peter 5:10, MLB, italics mine)."

What a comforting verse! My father-in-law, who lived twenty-five hundred miles away, had been in the Word and was prompted by the Holy Spirit to share that verse with us at exactly the perfect time.

Later I asked the Lord, *Is it possible that you will indeed equip, stabilize, strengthen, and establish us?* I wanted so desperately to believe that. I had nothing else to encourage me, so I clung to that promise. I was at the bottom of a deep well. The sides were so slippery that I could not climb out myself. It was as if the Lord reached down to where I was in that dark hole and pulled me out with his strong arm and with that verse.

> *I rejoice in your word like one who finds a great treasure.*
>
> **Psalm 119:162, NLT**

Not long after that phone call, both my husband and I began to feel the oppression lift. Our church had an incredible time of prayer one Sunday. Many people prayed for church unity and forgiveness, and we felt a renewed spirit among the congregation. We had new joy and enthusiasm; God's church was going forward. More than twenty-five years later, we are still pastoring in that same church.

I have learned the most about God and myself through difficult situations. At such times, God strips away all other comforts and crutches and teaches us to rely on him alone.

HEALING A PAST WOUND

As the tension within our church abated, the deep heart wound I still carried over the lack of relationship with my dad began to ache again. It was so deep that only the Lord Jesus could reach down far enough to remove the bitterness that had been growing over the years.

One evening as I was reading the book of Nehemiah, I came to these words: "Remember me with favor, O my God, for all I have done for these people" (Nehemiah 5:19). (Nehemiah had served as governor for twelve years.)

I laughed out loud. *Father,* I mused, *do you know what Nehemiah wanted from you? He wanted affirmation!* All of a sudden, I was stopped short by a voice inside my heart.

Yes, Marilyn, and that is exactly what you want—affirmation. You are not going to get that from your dad, but if you come to me I will affirm you.

Those words penetrated me very deeply. I was not used to the Holy Spirit speaking in a still, small voice. It was not an audible voice but rather an inner impression. I cannot explain exactly what happened in that moment, but as I was reading Scripture, the *Scripture read me!* I knew that I needed to forgive my dad for his years of neglect and abandonment in my life.

I began to weep. *Oh, Father, I do want his affirmation so badly. Every time I talk to my dad I always hope he will change. He never does. I understand that I cannot fix my dad. Lord Jesus, even though my dad may not be able to change, I can change with your help.*

Forgiveness began to wash over me. I had struggled to forgive my dad for years. Yet when I heard my heavenly Father speak those words to me, something broke free within me. It was cleansing; it was healing; and it was instantaneous. True, my dad hadn't changed, but I was different. The Lord began to replace my bitterness with compassion for my father. I had been waiting to *heal* first and then forgive him. The Lord showed me that I needed to heal by forgiving him first.

I was amazed at the way a passage of Scripture could bring such a major life change to me. That passage from Nehemiah doesn't even mention the topic of forgiveness. It was simply the Word and the Spirit of God moving powerfully in my thoughts and emotions.

God spoke his promises of healing to me through other verses as well: "The Lord is close to the brokenhearted and saves those who are crushed in spirit" (Psalm 34:18), and he stands "at the right hand of the needy one" (Psalm 109:31). I experienced firsthand Psalm 107:20: "He sent forth his word and healed them." When I was very needy, the Lord used his "living and active" Word to heal my damaged emotions (Hebrews 4:12). He extracted the root of bitterness within me.

By this point I realized that I could not live without the Word of God on a daily basis. God had shown me how his Word could help me with a large assignment, such as speaking to the teens. He'd also demonstrated that the Word could bring comfort during a rough church situation and healing to deep-seated bitterness. I had seen for myself how the Bible brought great hope in those crisis times. Now I was ready to see if God would speak to me from his Word in everyday, ordinary situations.

CHAPTER 2

God in the Ordinary

*L*ate one night as I was getting ready for bed, the phone rang. Wondering who could be calling at that odd time, I answered the phone and said hello. All I heard on the other end was hysterical crying. The caller was sobbing so hard that at first she couldn't even tell me who she was.

Finally, I was able to piece together her name and learn that she had just received a death threat. Naturally, she was terrified. She was crying so loudly that she drowned out my voice. "Listen," I finally shouted, "you have to hear this verse. 'But the Lord is faithful, and he will strengthen and protect you from the evil one.'" Suddenly I heard only silence on her end of the line.

"What did you just say?" she asked in a frightened voice.

I quietly repeated: "'But the Lord is faithful, and he will strengthen and protect you from the evil one.'"

Instantly she became calm. It was as if Jesus had told the tumultuous waves of fear inside of her to be still.

Where had the verse I quoted come from? That morning as I was reading in 2 Thessalonians, I felt prompted to stop and meditate on verse 3 of chapter 3. I sensed that I was supposed to share it with someone that day, although I didn't know whom. The parsonage phone rang incessantly, yet I did not feel led to share the verse with anyone who called. In fact, at ten o'clock that night I said to the Lord, "Well, that was a great verse you showed me this morning; I guess I'm just supposed to memorize it and share it with someone at another time." And then the final phone call came, and God used that same verse to bring peace to the caller's troubled spirit.

Once she had calmed down, we were able to talk about some options for her and pray together for her safety. After I hung up, I wondered what I would have said to her if the Lord had not shown me that verse earlier in the morning. I was amazed that God had used one Scripture verse to bring his great peace to someone else. I was also relieved to find out later that God protected her from her would-be attacker.

GOD'S PLANS FOR MY DAY

For many years I read the Bible simply for information and knowledge, not with the idea that God wanted to involve me in his plans for that day. When I took Joy's challenge to read the Bible daily, I determined that I would no longer read the Bible solely for *information,* but also for *transformation.* I wanted the word of Christ to dwell in me richly (Colossians 3:16). Up to that point, I had to admit, his Word had been dwelling in me quite poorly, because I never saw it as God's living communication with me.

Since the Bible was written under inspiration, I need to ask the Lord to help me read it by that same inspiration. When I read the Bible today, I don't try to find new revelations from God. Not at all! The Bible is complete. Rather, I ask God for application. What does he want me to do with his Word?

You see, God does work through ordinary people like you and me. All he requires is an open heart to hear what he is saying and to serve him as he directs. If we allow ourselves to be trained by the Word of God, we will be "thoroughly equipped for every good work" (2 Timothy 3:17).

Do you ever feel inadequate for a task? I certainly did when I first heard hysterical crying over the phone that night. Yet the Bible tells us that we can have confidence that the Lord will help and equip us as we allow God's Word to get into us. We then become an extension of Jesus Christ, the Living Word.

> *Blessed . . . are those who hear the word of God and obey it.*
> **Jesus, in Luke 11:28**

My friend Nancy told me a true story about a single mom who moved into an apartment complex with her children. One day while her children were swimming in the complex's pool, some older boys began bullying the children and calling them names. Frightened, the children ran to their apartment and told their mom what the boys were doing.

At this point, I probably would have gone upstairs to where those boys lived and told them to leave my children alone. This mother did an unusual thing, however. She gathered her kids and said, "Come on, let's get in the car and go to the store."

"The store?" they asked.

"Yes!" came their mom's reply. "We're going to go buy some stuff to make brownies and cookies."

They brought the ingredients home from the store and began baking. You can imagine the children's surprised faces when their mom announced that they were all going to take the treats up to the "mean boys" who lived on the third floor.

She knocked on the door and greeted one of the boys. "We're your new neighbors. We baked you some cookies and brownies. We like this apartment complex and just wanted to meet you." The boys were dumbfounded!

This mom had taken to heart Romans 12:17-19: "Do not

repay anyone evil for evil. Be careful to do what is right in the eyes of everybody. If it is possible, as far as it depends on you, live at peace with everyone. Do not take revenge, my friends." Great things happen when we get into the Scripture and allow the Scripture to get into us. God is able to work through us in ways that would be impossible in our own power. Discovering this truth is life changing!

PRAYING THE WORDS

Sometimes when I am reading the Bible, I discover the very words I need to pray for others. I recently spoke to a mom who was heartsick over the rebellion of her teen. Her son had gotten in with the wrong group at his high school, and he was headed in a downward spiral.

One morning after I had been praying earnestly for him, I began my daily Bible reading. I turned to Exodus and was surprised to see a verse that applied to this teen: "Do not follow the crowd in doing wrong" (Exodus 23:2). I stopped and prayed, *Father, this has been a problem for centuries! How current and up-to-date your Word is! You know what to do in these situations. Please help this young man to follow after you, not the crowd. Please bring someone godly alongside him.*

Another morning I came across Isaiah 29:24: "Those who are wayward in spirit will gain understanding; those who complain will accept instruction." By this time I had a list of the names of ten rebellious teens. I began to insert each of their names into that verse and pray, *Heavenly Father, please help _____ gain understanding and be willing to accept instruction.*

Praying Scripture is vital. When we do so, we actually pray God's Word back to him. You can begin by praying some of the recorded prayers in Scripture. The Lord's Prayer is recorded in Matthew 6:9-13. The apostle Paul's letters to the early churches contain many prayers as well.

Praying Scripture phrases and promises is powerful too. For

instance, you might pray, "Lord, thank you that your Word says you never leave us nor forsake us" (Hebrews 13:5). Praying Scripture reminds us who God is and brings us hope.

POWER IN THE BOOK
The power of God's Word really shouldn't surprise us when we consider all that it does.

>   It is the Book that gives purpose and meaning to
>   this life.
>   It is the Book that shows how we can have our sins
>   forgiven.
>   It is the Book that tells us how to get to heaven.
>   It is the Book that tells us how much God loves us.
>   It is the Book that talks about our relationship with God and
>   how the two of us can get together!
>   It is the Book that can bring hope to any situation.

This Book, unlike any other, is *always* on the best-seller list. What sets this Book apart from every other book is that it is *living!* No wonder God can and does speak through his Word— it is God-breathed!

In my early years of getting into the Word, 2 Timothy 3:16-17 had a profound impact on me: "*All* Scripture [and not just my favorite parts!] is God-breathed and is useful for teaching, rebuking, correcting and training in righteousness, *so that* the man of God may be thoroughly equipped for every good work" (emphasis mine).

If I wanted to know what the Lord desired to say to me and be prepared for him to work through me, I realized that I needed to allow his Word to do four things in my life: (1) teach, (2) rebuke, (3) correct, and (4) train in righteousness.

As I looked at those four words, the Lord spoke to my heart with these impressions:

We need the Bible to *teach* us so that we can know
what is right.
We need the Bible to *rebuke* us so that we can know
what is wrong.
We need the Bible to *correct* us so that we can know
how to get right.
We need the Bible to *train us in righteousness* so that
we can know *how to stay right.*

That verse has absolutely changed my life! I now read the Word asking God to work on me in those four areas. Some days I need correcting or rebuking. Other times I need teaching and training in righteousness. No matter what I need, God's Word seems to zero in on the area that needs work or encouragement.

"The word of God is full of *living power.* It is sharper than the sharpest knife, cutting deep into our innermost thoughts and desires. It exposes us for what we really are" (Hebrews 4:12, NLT, emphasis mine). I found that as I read this living Word, it was actually reading my attitudes.

Of course, some people say they don't like to read the Bible because it is just a list of dos and don'ts. The more I read, however, the more I realized that the Bible is not a rule book but a record of how God has reached out to people all through history.

Chuck Smith, founder of Calvary Chapel, uses the book of Ephesians to explain this idea. He notes that the first three chapters tell the church about the many spiritual blessings God has given them. Only in chapter 4 does Paul begin to discuss how Christians should live in light of all that God has done for them. "I found that when people began to discover who God is and all that God has done, they were eager to respond to God and did not have to be pushed or exhorted to pray or to serve. . . . They could not do enough for the Lord as they came to the recognition of what He had done for them."[1]

TEACHING THE WORD TO CHILDREN

When our daughter Abby was in fifth grade, I helped out on the playground during lunch recess. One day as Abby stood in a circle of girls, I watched as one of her classmates began passing out invitations to her birthday party. Since I was nearby, I noticed that all the girls in the circle received a party invitation—all the girls, that is, except Abby.

> *Every word of God is flawless; he is a shield to those who take refuge in him.*
>
> **Proverbs 30:5**

Oh no, I moaned quietly to myself. *This is going to be a problem.*

Sure enough, in a couple of minutes, Abby walked over to me. "Mom, I feel so bad—all the girls in my class but me got invitations to Kate's party! It makes me not want to invite her the next time I have a birthday party."

"I know, honey," I said, trying to console her.

As I drove home from the school's playground, I felt frustrated with Kate. Do you know what my "mother-heart" wanted to do when I saw my daughter excluded on the playground that day? I wanted to march right over to Kate and tell her that she was very insensitive. It was okay if my daughter wasn't invited to her party, but why did she have to pass out all the invitations in front of Abby? Couldn't her mom have mailed them? I fussed at God all the way back to my house.

When I finally allowed the Lord an opportunity to speak to my hard heart, this is what I sensed him saying: *Can you give up your right to feel hurt for your daughter and trust me instead? Are you going to allow resentment to build up against this girl so that every time you see her you think of this episode? Marilyn, do not fret! Do not pay back!*

Then the Lord reminded me of the passages from Proverbs and Psalms that I had read just that morning. I never realized I would have to put them into practice so soon! I opened my Bible and reread them.

Proverbs 20:22 cautions, "Do not say, 'I'll pay you back for this wrong!' Wait for the Lord, and he will deliver you." The passage from Psalms spoke to this situation as well: "Do not fret because of evil men. . . . Refrain from anger and turn from wrath; do not fret—it leads only to evil" (Psalm 37:1, 8). Ouch! These verses applied not only to Abby, but to me as well.

When Abby came home from school, she was still bothered by the event at recess. I could see the anger flashing in her eyes, and her normally soft heart had begun to stiffen. She wanted revenge—to return evil for evil. We talked for a while, and then I asked her to look at the verses I had read that morning. "It's understandable that you feel humiliated right now. But let me show you what God says about situations just like yours."

Two weeks later, when I was back on playground duty at Abby's school, one of her classmates came up to me and said, "Mrs. Hontz, be glad Abby did not go to Kate's party last Friday night! One girl came to the party with the stomach flu and everyone ended up getting it except for me." (The next day this girl came down with the flu too.)

Now, let me quickly add that the Lord did *not* give them the stomach flu because they did not invite Abby. However, Abby learned some important lessons from all of this. She saw, through her ten-year-old eyes, that the Lord was indeed watching out for her. He spared her from getting the stomach flu, for which she was very grateful. She also learned that she needed to let the Lord work out hurtful situations, especially when there was nothing she could do about them. I would have missed that mentoring time with my daughter if I had failed to read the Word that morning. I also would have missed hearing the Holy Spirit check my *own* attitude.

My heart's desire was to teach our children to read the Bible daily, so they could see what God might want to show them for that specific day. I yearned for them to understand the concept that the Bible could teach, rebuke, correct, and train them too—

that they would know what is right, what is wrong, how to get right, and how to stay right. I wanted them to be able to read the Bible so God would speak to their hearts.

One evening, while tucking our nine-year-old son in bed, I noticed big tears starting to flow down his cheeks. "Paul, what's the matter?" I asked.

"Mom, I did something wrong," he said quietly.

"Tell me about it, Paul," I gently coaxed.

"I wrote in my reading log at school that I read for an hour, but I really only read for thirty minutes."

"So what are you telling me, honey?" I asked.

"I lied to my teacher about my reading log."

We talked a little more about the situation. My husband came in to say good night to Paul, and our son related his sin to his dad.

"You know what this means, don't you, Son?" my husband said.

"Yes, Dad. I need to ask the Lord to forgive me. I also need to tell my teacher tomorrow that I lied and cheated on my reading log. I will have to ask him to forgive me."

We agreed with Paul and then prayed with him. Following Paul's confession to the Lord, my husband said, "Paul, if you'd like, I will go to school tomorrow at lunchtime while you tell your teacher what you did. I won't say anything; I'll just stand next to you. Do you want me to come?"

"Yes, I'd like that, Dad," he responded gratefully.

The next morning as I read my Bible, I came across Proverbs 12:22: "The Lord detests lying lips, but he delights in men who are truthful." I smiled as I read that verse. How appropriate that was for Paul's situation! I wrote the verse on a three by five card and decided to share it with Paul before he went to school.

After we agreed that the verse says that God hates lying, I said, "Listen carefully to what the rest of the verse says: 'He delights in men who are truthful.' Right now, Paul, God is delighting in you because you told the truth and you want to make a wrong right."

A huge smile spread across his face. "Mom, could I please have that card with the verse on it? I'd like to keep it in my backpack today." I gladly handed him the card.

TRAINING MANUAL

I'm not suggesting that we hit others over the head with the Bible every time they sin. We do, however, want to use God's Word at the appropriate time. This is especially true when it comes to our own children. The Bible is the best parenting book out there. Our children *do* come with a "manual" when they are born—God's Word. It is our responsibility to know it and practice its principles. It truly does teach, rebuke, correct, and train us, as well as our children.

Reading the Bible with one of my children convinced me that God has a sense of humor. The night before our second-oldest daughter, Holly, turned sixteen, I suggested she begin to read a chapter of Proverbs each night and look for what God might want to say to her. Though her mind was focused on the driver's license she would receive the following day, she decided to end that evening with some quiet time.

Not long after she went to her room, I heard her laughing. "Mom," she called, "come to my room! You won't believe this!"

I found her sitting up on her bed with her Bible open. "I want to show you what I think the Lord wants me to know before I get my driver's license tomorrow," she said. "Look what I just read in Proverbs: 'Do not swerve to the right or the left; keep your foot from evil' (Proverbs 4:27)."

We decided right then that God had sent her a "prelicense reproof" through that verse. All joking aside, that is the night that Holly committed to read God's Word in a new way—until God spoke to her heart.

As I regularly spent time reading God's Word, I discovered

that God did want to speak to me about the trivial, everyday events of my life, as well as provide direction and comfort when I was faced with major decisions and hurt. I discovered that he used his Word to actively demonstrate his love to others and to smooth the rough edges in my own life.

What I have learned about listening boils down to this: The primary way for each of us to recognize God's voice is to read the Word of God regularly. *If we want to recognize God's voice, we must be in the Word every day.*

CHAPTER 3

Finding God in His Word

*A*s a child, I worried that while in bed at night a big arm might reach out from under my bed and grab me. I made sure none of my body parts hung over the side of my bed!

I also worried that my mother would die. She and I had many conversations about this—even before she was diagnosed with cancer.

I remember talking with my mother about my "worry problem" when I was a young child. She told me that only one kind of person was allowed to worry. I was encouraged, thinking I would probably fit into that category.

I asked her, "Who is allowed to worry?"

She replied, "Only non-Christians may worry. They don't realize that they have a heavenly Father who will take care of them."

Despite my mother's counsel, my tendency to worry continued into adulthood. One day I was reading Philippians 4:6: "Don't worry about anything; instead, pray about everything" (TLB). All of a sudden the word *anything* hit me—I was not supposed to worry about anything! The Bible does not say *try* not to worry about anything; it says, "Don't worry about anything." That was not just a polite saying—it was a command from the Lord.

What was I supposed to do? I was a worrier! God used that verse to show me that worrying was something I was not created to do. In fact, it was a sin for me to do so. I realized I had a choice—either I was going to continue worrying or allow the Lord to help me overcome this tendency.

My mother tried to help me stop worrying, and I'm glad she did. However, it was the convicting power of God's Word that eventually brought lasting change. Something powerful happens when God speaks personally to us through his Word.

Of course, that will not happen if we don't take the time to open God's Word and begin to digest it. "Solid food is for the mature, who by *constant* use have trained themselves to distinguish good from evil" (Hebrews 5:14, emphasis mine).

GETTING STARTED

Obviously, the way you structure your time in the Word may differ from my approach. Yet if you have recently committed to spending more time in God's Word, I'd like to offer some practical suggestions to help you as you get started.

Get the right tools. Choose a Bible that you find very readable. I often recommend the New Living Translation, which was translated thought for thought instead of word for word. Many have told me how that version has increased their understanding of the Word. Perhaps you prefer the New King James Version, the New American Standard Version, or the New International Version. The important thing is that you read it as Ezra, an Old Testament prophet, did. The Bible tells us that he "had *disciplined* himself to *study* the Law of the Lord, to *practice* it, and to *teach* its statues and ordinances in Israel" (Ezra 7:10, MLB, emphasis mine).

You might consider purchasing a commentary, a Bible dictionary, or a Bible with study notes. These can be helpful when you come across a term or passage that you don't understand or for which you want more insight. (For more suggestions on choosing a Bible and study tools, see appendix A.)

> *This is the one I esteem: he who is humble and contrite in spirit, and trembles at my word.*
> **Isaiah 66:2**

Be willing to mark up your Bible with a pen or highlighter that will not bleed through the pages of your Bible. I encourage you to write notes in the margins and put the date by verses that speak to you at a certain time in your life.

Decide on a place. Try to find a place to read the Bible where you will be free of distractions. You might go consistently to the same spot, or perhaps you'd prefer to vary your solitary place. For me, it helps to go to the same place each day to help set the pattern.

Keep pens, notebooks, a journal, tissues, and whatever else you will need at your designated place. That way it will always be ready for you.

Determine a time. You may notice that it is so much easier to find time to read the newspaper, books, magazines, and e-mail or watch television. That is why it is so important to *make* time to read the Bible. It just won't happen otherwise.

Ask the Lord to show you a time slot in your day to read the Bible. For the first four years that I read the Word regularly, I read at night. I was a "night person" and our house was quieter at that time. Gradually, with the Lord's help, I switched my reading time to the morning. This worked better for me, because I found I was able to use what I read throughout the day. However, each person needs to determine a schedule that works best for him or her.

Do it daily. Occasionally people tell me that they know they should be in the Bible on a consistent basis, but they just can't find the time to do it. Yet, I know that these same people would not think about going out of the house without brushing their teeth. Even though we know we should look to God's Word each day, many of us put other things first. May I challenge you to discover the depths of God on a daily basis? May I challenge you to read the Bible every day, until the day you die? If you begin to read the Bible daily to see what God will say to you, you will not want to live one day without it.

"Each day," my father-in-law often says, "you do what you want to do." It's true. Everyone has been given twenty-four hours each day, and most days we have the freedom to decide how to use these hours. Suppose you come home to discover a dinner invitation. If you were tired, you might be tempted to decline. However, if your host said he had some inheritance money to pass on to you that evening, you would go, no matter how tired you were. Likewise, if you are serious about discovering the treasures in God's Word, you must open your Bible. God will be faithful to do his work in you daily.

Pray for a desire to read the Word. Ask the Lord to make you "hungry" for his Word—to increase your appetite. As you begin to "taste and see that the Lord is good" (Psalm 34:8), you will hunger for more. I mentioned that when I began reading the Bible, I read until I sensed the Holy Spirit pointing out a verse or passage for me. I then wrote that Scripture in my journal. Now, however, even if a verse speaks to me, I often go on reading because I want to. My desire is to read through the Bible as many times as I can.

Beware, however, of the lethargy that can creep in if you start neglecting your time in the Word. What usually happens when you skip lunch or dinner? You get hungry, right? I have found that the same is not true if I skip a spiritual "meal." The longer I stay away from the Bible, the less I feel hunger pangs. That is why I pray, *Lord, make me hungry for you and your Word.*

I like how the prophet Jeremiah put it, "When your words came, I ate them; they were my joy and my heart's delight" (Jeremiah 15:16).

I believe that when I stand before my heavenly Father one day I will ask myself, *Why didn't I read the Word more? Why didn't I spend more time getting to know him on earth?*

Ask for the Holy Spirit's leading. Keep in mind that the Bible was written under the Holy Spirit's inspiration. Ask the Lord to help you read it under that same inspiration. Ask him to speak to your heart as you read.

Read the Bible for transformation, not just for information. In other words, read for change and not just knowledge. Head knowledge is important; however, the Bible should affect the heart as well. After you read the Word, you should be able to identify a change you need to make or a practical insight you've gained.

LISTEN FOR GOD'S VOICE

You are reading Scripture, not to check off a box on your to-do list, but to connect personally and directly with your Creator and Savior. The following suggestions are practices that have helped me to hear God's voice while reading the Bible.

Look for the connections among Scripture passages. Work through the Scriptures systematically so that you can see how the Old and New Testaments together reveal God's master plan. Each day I read one portion from the Old Testament and one from the New Testament. In doing so, I often discover links between Old Testament and New Testament passages.

For example, I recently finished reading the song of Moses and Miriam, which they sang after the Lord parted the Red Sea as the Israelites fled Egypt (Exodus 15). A few days later I came to Revelation 15:2-3 in my New Testament reading: "They held harps given them by God and sang the song of Moses the servant of God and the song of the Lamb."

There again was that phrase, the "song of Moses." I went

back to Exodus 15 and reread it. How blessed I was to see that connection and to be reminded that our God "will reign for ever and ever" (Exodus 15:18). He was not only victorious during the time of Moses, but he will one day be the victorious Lamb over all.

Put yourself in Scripture. As you read, try to picture yourself in the scene. For example, as you read about Jesus preaching to the masses, imagine yourself being jostled by the huge crowds as they press toward Jesus. Let the Lord use your imagination—he created it. Visualizing the story will give you a greater understanding of what it means and how it should impact your life.

Put Scripture into practice. Ask yourself questions like: *What does this mean for me? How does this relate to my life? What do I need to do with what I just read?* Resolve not only to read the Bible every day, but to live it out as well. James 1:22 says, "Do not merely listen to the word, and so deceive yourselves. *Do what it says*" (emphasis mine). Most of us know what the Bible teaches us to do. Our problem lies in the day-to-day living out of the principles.

The apostle Paul reminds us to "live up to what we have already attained" (Philippians 3:16). I remember the first time that verse struck me. I asked the Lord, *What teachings do I already know that need to be lived out in my life?*

Put others into the Scripture. As you read, look for Scriptures that will not only encourage you but others as well. I once read a verse from Isaiah that brought great comfort to me: "For I am the Lord, your God, who takes hold of your right hand and says to you, Do not fear; I will help you" (Isaiah 41:13). I knew it was too good to keep to myself.

Many times since then I have shared that verse with people who are fearful. I ask them to picture Jesus taking their right hand. Then I say, "Listen to the Lord say to you, 'Do not fear; I will help you.'" It is one thing for me to tell others not to be afraid; it is quite another if God whispers to their frightened heart. That verse is comforting and power-filled!

Write down verses. Whenever a verse captures your attention, jot it down. This will help solidify the verse in your mind. A couple of months ago, as I was working my way through Ephesians, I came to a verse that stopped me as clearly as if I had come to a red light. How could such a short verse do that? It simply says: "Find out what pleases the Lord" (Ephesians 5:10). That was it—a little verse, but a big concept.

I found myself applying it over and over throughout my day. In fact, it is still impacting me. It comes to mind often, especially when I am praying: *Lord Jesus, help me to find out what pleases you in this situation.*

Memorize Scripture. When the Lord uses a verse to get your attention, try to memorize it. Memorizing will help you internalize the Scripture. The Holy Spirit is able to bring to your mind a verse at just the right time. My husband pointed out recently that when Jesus was alone in the wilderness being tempted by Satan, he only had one weapon—the memorized Word of God (see Matthew 4:1-11).

Right now I am memorizing Psalm 63:1-8, which begins: "O God, you are my God; I earnestly search for you" (NLT). I chose this passage because I am more aware than ever of my deep need for God.

Journal as you read. In 1982, when my friend Joy first encouraged me to read the Bible every day, she suggested that I journal the verse or verses that were meaningful to me. Little did I know then that journaling verses would prove to be the hook that kept me connected to the Word. I am more disciplined to find Scripture that speaks to me if I know I am going to write it down. Journaling Scripture also helps me retain the verse through my day.

There are many ways to journal, but here are some practices that have helped me. I use a small legal tablet that fits in the inside cover of my Bible. That way it is always available when I see something from the Word that I want to write down. I begin every journal entry with the date; then I write "Dear Father." I write down the verse that he has "highlighted" for me for that day. I then write to him about what that verse means to me. When I sense the Lord speaking to me about the verse, I write down those thoughts right away. If I don't, it is harder to go back and capture the essence of those first thoughts.

Some people write journals for their eyes only. I prefer to write them so that my children may read them. Your entries can become a "spiritual inheritance" that you pass down to your children. My mother did that for me and my siblings, and they are cherished keepsakes for us.

This spiritual inheritance can take different forms. At age twenty, a year before he met me, my husband wrote a beautiful letter to the Lord expressing the desire of his heart. He wrote about the wife he would like to marry—including a list of ten specific qualities! I have that letter in our cedar chest, and it is a treasured legacy. Someday I will share it with our son.

On the birthday of each of my children, I journal how I see my child growing spiritually at that age. I also record the ways I see God working in his or her life. Our children know they may pick up my journal and look up the entry for their birthday. Years from now I would like them to recall how I saw them at a particular age and what my spiritual goals for them were. By journaling their spiritual progress, I also know better how to pray for them. You may also want to do this for your grandchildren or other children in your family.

I seek to keep the journal entries positive. That does not mean I don't share anything negative—I desire to be transparent. I share as honestly as I can and admit when I am going through a tough situation. However, I want to weave threads of hope and trust throughout those pages no matter what has happened.

On really rough days—especially times when I cannot talk

over a situation with anyone—I write out all my feelings. I then ask the Lord to show me a verse or a promise that I can write across the page. Next, I rip it out, tear it up, and throw it away. Journaling can be very therapeutic!

After I journal to the Lord, I pause and ask him if there is anything he would like to say to me. Often, though not every day, the Holy Spirit will speak to my heart in that silent time. I recognize his voice because it is always consistent with Scripture and it

> *Heaven and earth will pass away, but my words will never pass away.*
> **Jesus, in Matthew 24:35**

brings peace to my soul. When he does speak, I write down what I sense the Lord is saying to me.

Let me give you an example. Recently I was mediating on Ephesians 2:10: "For we are God's workmanship, created in Christ Jesus to do good works, which God prepared in advance for us to do." I wrote the verse and then continued writing: "Heavenly Father, help me to grasp that I am your workmanship. I have been belittling myself so much lately. I keep saying, 'I can't do this' and 'I'm not good enough to do that.' My self-talk has been pretty negative lately, Father. Please remind me that I am created by you to do good works."

I then wrote down as the Father responded with specific words: "My child, if only you would focus on me instead of your weaknesses. Yes, you may be weak, but I am strong. You can do all things through me, because I strengthen you. You are my workmanship, my doing. I have good works for you to do. No one can do them except you. These are works that I planned in advance for you to do. Please know, Marilyn, that I have *never* put a pessimistic thought in your mind. Be on guard, for they come from the enemy of your soul. Don't believe his lies. Let me help you with your self-talk. Remember who you are in me—you are my creation, my workmanship. I love you, my child."

You may be thinking, *Well that's okay for you, but I don't like to write, let alone journal.* May I encourage you to try it? Journal once a week by simply writing down a verse that God is seeking to work into the fabric of your life. If something strikes you about the verse, write that down too. I cannot tell you how meaningful my mother's journals are to me at this stage in my life. I want to carry on her tradition. It's not too late to start that same tradition for your family.

If you are a man who is thinking, *That journaling stuff is for women,* remember that the book of Psalms is full of journals written by men. King David wrote in his "journal": "One generation will commend your works to another; they will tell of your mighty acts" (Psalm 145:4).

One last thought on journaling: To whom do you talk the most? Perhaps your spouse, a parent, a sibling, or your closest friend comes to mind. Maybe you think you talk most to the Lord. Actually, I believe that the one we talk to the most is our *self.* May I challenge you to write down that self-talk and then seek the Lord's help to overcome negative thinking? (He knows all of our thoughts anyway.) God has a wonderful way of taking the thoughts we write on paper and reflecting his thoughts back to us. If we have "stinking thinking," he can set us straight. Allow the Holy Spirit to work through your written words with his written Word.

Keep at it. If you miss a day of reading the Word, don't get discouraged. My husband often tells people who want to get back into spending time with the Lord, "It's never too late to start again." The Lord emphasizes this in both the Old and New Testaments. "Return to me, and I will return to you" (Malachi 3:7). "Come near to God and he will come near to you" (James 4:8).

Find an accountability partner. Staying in the Word will be easier if you have a friend to help keep you accountable. If you do not have such a person, ask the Lord to bring someone into your life. My friend Joy was a good catalyst for me; however, we lived too far apart to meet regularly. Don't get discouraged if you don't find someone right away. When you find that person, it will have been worth the wait!

Welcome godly friends who dare to ask you the hard questions in life. I need people to ask, "Marilyn, what are you reading in the Word these days? What is God teaching you through those passages?" Those kinds of questions help fan the spiritual sparks in my life so they don't die down. My husband and I are involved in a small group where the members ask us these and other questions each month. I have learned that we really do need each other.

How enjoyable it is to talk with someone who reads Scripture consistently. I have been amazed to see how often God works through the same Scripture to speak to me and to others. Many times the Spirit has shown me a specific verse for my day and I later discover that he has put the same verse on the heart of my mentor, Kathleen, who lives twenty-five hundred miles away!

Recently Kathleen and I were both in what we called "the ash heap." She was dealing with a difficult ministry issue, and I was discouraged about a staff situation. She called me to tell me that the Lord had shown her a verse that she had taken to heart. When she recited the verse, "I command you—be strong and courageous! Do not be afraid or discouraged. For the Lord your God is with you wherever you go" (Joshua 1:9, NLT), I gasped. It was the exact verse that I had read that morning. In fact, I had circled the word *discouraged.*

This happens frequently! At times when Kathleen and I are praying for a mutual friend, the Lord leads both of us to the same verse to pray for that friend. We believe this is the Holy Spirit helping us to know how to pray.

PEOPLE OF THE BOOK
Evangelist and reformer John Wesley once said, "Let me be a man of one Book."[2] Would you like to be a "person of the

Book"? It will happen only if you embrace the discipline of daily Bible reading. As a former Sunday school teacher of mine said, "I have never met anyone flourishing in his or her spiritual life who is not enmeshed in the Word of God."

I know I enjoy being around people who have made God's Word a priority in their life. I've noticed that these people seem less ruffled when a crisis arises. They still have problems and concerns, but they aren't as caught off guard as others are. They seem to have an underlying sense of peace. I've also noticed that other people like to be around these "people of the Book." Why? I think it is because they are more Christlike. Such people desire to be "imitators of God" (Ephesians 5:1). How can we be imitators of God for our children, grandchildren, and others if we are not reading the Word?

The physical world provides a good illustration of what it takes to be passionate for God. In order for water to change properties and turn to steam, it must be heated to a temperature of 212° F. The heat must stay consistently at that temperature for it to keep boiling. If the heat is lowered, the boiling stops. Consistency of temperature is absolutely necessary for boiling. So, too, is my consistency in reading the Word of God necessary to keep me "hot" for God. I can't allow myself to lose the "steam" in my reading of the Word.

What will it take for us to be hot for God? Others around us are going to be affected by our "spiritual temperature," either for good or ill. What is it going to take for us to raise our passion for God's Word even one degree?

Sometimes I believe the enemy of our soul tempts us with the thought that, even if we try, we won't be able to keep our steam in consistently reading the Word of God. He will try to keep you from attempting a deeper walk by using the excuse that you will probably fail. This is a lie!

Start where you are now. Set aside a time to read the Word today. Even if you start with the smallest step, the Lord Jesus, the living Word, will be there to meet you. You will find that God's daily Word to you will help prepare you for your day. He *will* speak to your heart. You will recognize your Father's voice through the reading of the Bible. Remember, God's Word stands forever!

> *The grass withers and the flowers fall, but the word of our God stands forever.*
>
> **Isaish 40:8**

This morning, the very day I had planned to finish this section on recognizing God's voice while reading Scripture, I "just happened" to read a passage from Revelation that illustrates the power of the Word of God: "I saw heaven standing open and there before me was a white horse, whose rider is called Faithful and True. With justice he judges and makes war. His eyes are like blazing fire, and on his head are many crowns. He has a name written on him that no one knows but he himself. He is dressed in a robe dipped in blood, and his name is the *Word of God*" (Revelation 19:11-13, emphasis mine). Oh, the privilege of getting to know Jesus, who is himself the Word of God, *now*, here on earth!

QUESTIONS TO THINK ABOUT

1. What are some times in your life when the Bible has helped to *teach* you, *rebuke* you, *correct* you, or *train you in righteousness*? What promise are you given in 2 Timothy 3:16-17 if you allow yourself to be trained by the Word of God?
2. When was the last time you heard God speak as you read Scripture? How did the message impact you or someone else?
3. What barriers keep you from reading Scripture consistently? What steps could you take to become more consistent in spending time in God's Word?
4. Which of the suggestions in chapter 3 on listening for God's voice might you try to help you go deeper into the Bible?
5. How do you think spending time each day in God's Word would affect the way you plan your days?
6. Do you know anyone whom you consider a "person of the Book"? If so, what do you notice in his or her approach to life that is different from most people's?
7. Read Romans 12:9-21 very slowly, as if you were reading it for the first time. Ask the Holy Spirit if there is a word or a phrase he would like to highlight for you, and ask him to speak to your heart as you read this passage. This is a great way to learn how to recognize the voice of the Lord.

Recognizing God's Voice While Praying

PART 2

CHAPTER 4

"Lord, Teach Me to Pray"

*F*our years after beginning the practice of reading Scripture daily, I had an encounter with Jesus while reading the Bible that revealed another deep need in my life: a daily prayer time.

One summer morning I read the familiar story of Jesus' bringing his disciples with him to the Garden of Gethsemane following their final Passover celebration together (see Matthew 26:36-46).

He called three of them, Peter, James, and John, to walk ahead with him. He confided to them that his soul was "crushed with grief to the point of death." He then asked them to "stay here and watch with me" (Matthew 26:38, NLT).

After going a little farther alone, Jesus fell to his face and agonized before his Father in prayer. When Jesus returned to the three disciples, he found them asleep.

"Could you not watch with Me one hour?" he asked (Matthew 26:40, NKJV).

Come on, disciples! I wanted to shout. *Jesus just told you his gut feelings; don't you care? If a friend of mine expressed such sadness, I'd be right there for him!*

My accusations stopped when I heard the Holy Spirit ask me that same question: *Marilyn, can you watch with me for one hour?*

Suddenly, I was standing in the Garden of Gethsemane, watching Jesus desperately seeking someone to pray with him. It was a powerful image.

In the garden, the disciples did not comprehend the importance of prayer or how much Jesus wanted them to join him in intercession. And neither, I realized, did I.

Oh, sure, I prayed at mealtimes, but I did not have a specific time to pray daily. Many times I did not pray unless I was desperate. Generally, I thought I could work things out on my own. With that attitude, it's not surprising that my prayer time was "hit and miss" and lacked passion.

The Bible makes it clear that prayer is very important to God. He does not see it merely as a religious activity, but as a means for him to build a relationship with us. And as difficult as we sometimes find it to make time for prayer, it required an infinitely greater sacrifice from him. "Beware of placing the emphasis on what prayer costs us," said author Oswald Chambers. "It cost God everything to make it possible for us to pray."[3] Paul explained that we have access to the Father only because of Jesus' death and resurrection: "Because of Christ and our faith in him, we can now come fearlessly into God's presence, assured of his glad welcome" (Ephesians 3:12, NLT).

As I became more interested in prayer, I had to contend with some puzzling questions. God doesn't need anything from me since he is all-powerful, so why does it matter whether I pray? Why tell God my needs when he already knows them?

I have learned that the only way to gain insight into these questions is to pray. It was as I prayed that my questions gave way to this bottom-line answer: We pray because God wants to be in relationship with us! He simply desires for us to communicate with him and allow him to communicate with us. Scripture says that Jesus lives to make intercession for us (Hebrews 7:25). He chooses to pray. Prayer is our way of choosing to show God that we too value this relationship.

This past summer my daughter Mandy and son-in-law John interned together at a church. They spent most days working together. Since they witnessed what each was doing, did they really need time to talk about their work? John told me, "After a month or so we realized we still needed to ask each other about our day, simply for the sake of connection. Without a daily debriefing time, we felt disconnected, though we both already knew about each other's day." Likewise, God knows our needs, but we connect with him when we open our hearts to him.

Let's say you watch your son make a touchdown during a high school football game. You see him score, you cheer for him along with the crowd, but there is something extraspecial when your son tells you about that play after the game. In fact, you encourage him to do so. What kid wouldn't love to have that focused attention? What parent doesn't love that kind of interaction? God is watching us all the time yet says, *Tell me about it.*

God also desires us to pray because through prayer:

- We acknowledge our dependency on him.
- We grow in grace and humility.
- Our relationship with God is enriched.
- We come to understand his will for us.
- We see our inability to control situations.
- We view God's mercies as answers to prayer rather than coincidence.
- God can pour out his comfort and peace in the midst of tragedy and hopelessness.
- We are changed.

While there are many reasons to pray, one other is particularly meaningful to me: God collects our prayers. According to Revelation 5:8 and 8:3-4, God saves them and considers them to be a sweet fragrance offered to him. It's as if he saves all these "love letters" addressed to him.

Although our prayers are vital to us, they are also, mysteriously, important to God. Scripture is full of times when prayers affected him.

The prophet Isaiah told King Hezekiah he was going to die. The king pleaded with God to allow him to live longer. God heard his prayers and allowed Hezekiah to live another fifteen years (2 Kings 20:1-6).

God listened to Elijah when he asked that it not rain for three and a half years. When Elijah asked for rain, God sent it (1 Kings 17–18). In fact, James used this example to illustrate the power of prayer (James 5:17-18). "The prayer of a righteous person is powerful and effective" (James 5:16, TNIV).

DEVOTED TO PRAYER

Considering the great value God places on prayer, it is no surprise that he continued to nudge me in this area. The Holy Spirit used other Scripture passages to draw me to prayer. In Colossians 4:2, I read the command to "*devote* yourselves to prayer" (emphasis mine). That was definitely not me. I was devoted to my husband and to my children, but devoted to prayer? No way.

The prophet Isaiah lamented the Israelites' lack of prayer when he cried out to God, "No one calls on your name or strives to lay hold of you" (Isaiah 64:7). I realized I fit that category. I was not calling on the name of the Lord.

One day during my Bible reading, I read about King Amaziah of Judah, whose reign is summed up in 2 Chronicles 25:2: He "did what was pleasing in the Lord's sight, *but not wholeheartedly*" (NLT, emphasis mine). Because of this, the king's reign ended in his defeat and assassination. Much of the trouble began when he turned to idols and stopped listening for the voice of God. I did not want to make the same mistake and continue with a half-hearted prayer life. I knew that I needed to be totally, wholeheartedly devoted to God in prayer.

> *Jesus often withdrew to lonely places and prayed.*
> Luke 5:16

Then I read about the prophet Samuel. He modeled what it means to be devoted to prayer. He told the Israelites: "As for me, far be it from me that I should sin against the Lord by failing to pray for you" (1 Samuel 12:23). Samuel took prayer seriously. He saw it as a sin to neglect praying for his countrymen. I am sure he prayed for King Saul too. After reading that passage, I realized I did not pray regularly for my country or for those in authority over me.

As I meditated on that verse, I also realized I wasn't praying for those in my care. The Lord spoke to my heart again: *Marilyn, nobody will pray more for your children than you!* Our children were ten, eight, five, and eighteen months old at that time. I had not been praying consistently for them, and that bothered me.

I had been confronted with the "active" Word of God. Now, what was I going to do with the truth that had convicted me? I found myself asking (as the disciples did in Luke 11:1), *Jesus, would you please teach me to pray?*

The Lord used a woman from our church to start me on my journey of prayer. When I mentioned that I had a desire to pray but lacked the motivation, Martha loaned me book after book on ordinary people who had become mighty people of prayer. The first book I read was the life story of George Müller, a nineteenth-century evangelist and founder of a number of orphanages and schools in Great Britain. He is perhaps best known for his vibrant prayer life, for this man depended solely on God through prayer to bring food to the orphanages he ran.

My husband introduced me to the works of E. M. Bounds, a

nineteenth-century minister and Civil War chaplain who wrote extensively on prayer. Each day he spent the early morning hours on his knees in prayer. I marveled at how people like him lived full, dynamic lives simply because they prayed. Their lives were not easy, but they had learned to trust their heavenly Father for every need. They experienced an abundance of peace.

Surprisingly, reading their stories did not make me feel guilty. Instead, I felt a deep sense of loss in my life. I obviously was missing out on something incredible. My hunger intensified.

DRIVEN TO PRAYER

Circumstances also began driving my desire for intimate prayer time with God. In fact, it seems that the best time for the Lord to teach me anything is when I am desperate for him. That is how I felt during the summer of l986.

After suffering a stroke, my dad had been placed in a nursing home twenty-five hundred miles away in California. I flew from Michigan with our toddler, Abby, to visit him. As I stood by his bedside, he begged me to take him back to his house.

"Marilyn, please take me home," he cried out over and over. His blue eyes pleaded with me as he gripped my hand. It was heart wrenching.

"Dad, I'm so sorry, but I can't. You have to stay here where you can get the help you need."

I felt like my dad and I had reversed roles. He was the child and I was the parent. What was I to do? He needed total care and his wife could not lift and care for him at home. My brother had offered to move them to Michigan, but they did not want to leave California.

Finally, his begging changed to: "I want to go home to heaven."

I held Abby tightly in my lap on the plane ride home. Thoughts swirled around my head and heart. *What are my siblings and I supposed to do?* I asked again. I felt guilty knowing my dad didn't want to be in a nursing home. I felt sad because we lived so far apart and I couldn't visit him as much as he would have liked. And I felt shame because I thought children were supposed to be able to help their aging parents. I knew we needed the Lord to guide us. I needed to pray.

I wanted to become a person of prayer like Epaphras. He was one of the apostle Paul's prayer partners. When Paul wrote a letter to the people in Colossae, he described Epaphras this way: "He is always wrestling in prayer for you" (Colossians 4:12).

"Always wrestling"? I asked myself. *What does it mean to "wrestle" in prayer?* Whatever it meant, I knew I was not doing it.

At the same time I was concerned about my dad, I felt overwhelmed by a conflict with a friend. We couldn't seem to work out our differences, no matter how many times we talked. That too drove me to prayer.

Finally, through convicting Scripture verses, books on prayer, and difficult circumstances, the Holy Spirit had helped me catch the much needed spirit of prayer. Now I was ready to begin.

MAKING TIME FOR PRAYER

The pressing question, as I began planning a regular time of prayer, was *when* I was going to pray. I got up each morning (at the very last second) in time to feed the baby, make our other three children breakfast, pack three sack lunches, and get the kids to the school bus on time. I had it down to the wire, but I was very frazzled. I sensed the Lord telling me that it didn't need to be that way.

But Father, I cannot get up any earlier. You know that the baby has me up several times a night. I am so tired and so busy, I complained.

The Lord, however, continued to nudge me to get up earlier. It was the only time for me to have moments of peace and quiet. Once our kids and dog were up and the parsonage phone began to ring, it was bedlam. God seemed to say that if I made time for him, he would help me with the remaining hours of my day. I decided that just as spending time in the Word was a choice, so was prayer. It was up to me.

I also had to admit that I had noticed a common thread in the biographies of prayer warriors. Most of them had regular early morning appointments with the Lord. Furthermore, many prayed for extended periods of time.

Early American Methodist bishop Francis Asbury got up at 4 A.M. and spent two hours in prayer and meditation. Seventeenth-century preacher and theologian Samuel Rutherford rose at three in the morning to meet God in prayer. John Welch, a Scottish preacher, spent eight or ten hours in prayer at a time, saying that he had "the souls of three thousand to answer for, and I know not how it is with many of them!" One prayer warrior and minister named Edward Payson spent much time in secret prayer. He actually wore grooves into the hardwood floorboards because his knees pressed against them so often and so long.[4] Wow, "knee prints"!

Finally, in early August 1986, I decided that beginning in September, I would try to get up an hour earlier than usual. (I loved sleeping in on summer mornings and did not want to give up that extra sleep time.) In September the older children would be back in school, and I would not have the luxury of sleeping in anyway. What a major shift this was going to be for a busy, disorganized, and undisciplined mom.

On September 5 my alarm went off at 6 A.M. For the first time in my life, I dragged myself out of bed early to pray. I stubbed my toe on the footboard of the bed and groggily limped down the stairs to the laundry room. The mountains of laundry seemed to say, "We've been waiting for you; where have you been?"

Father, you are going to have to help me pray, I began. *I feel like I need toothpicks to prop open my eyelids.*

I prayed—my first request concerned my dad's situations—

and in five minutes I was done! I had prayed about everything I could think of. I had truly expected that it would be simple to pray for an hour. After all, if the Lord asked his disciples to do it, it couldn't be so hard, could it?

But I found that prayer was hard labor. There was no way that I could watch for one hour.

"This will never work," I said out loud. Then I remembered my friend Joy's voice saying, "Try it for twenty-one days."

"But it is so hard," I whimpered.

Then it dawned on me that my laundry was not the only thing waiting for me in the laundry room. The Lord Jesus himself was waiting for me every morning. When I was able to picture Jesus standing in my laundry room waiting for me because *he* wanted to be with me, it blew me away! I truly believe that if we could grasp how much the Lord loves us and desires us, we would not miss an opportunity to meet with him. Guess where I discovered that the Lord loves you and me so much? It happened in my time in the laundry room, tucked away, alone with him.

Every day I made myself get up early. It was not easy at first. I dreaded the alarm clock going off. *My body was not made to get up this early,* I mentioned to the Lord. I even told him that my stomach felt sick when I got up that early.

In my devotions, however, verses about prayer kept coming at me. I smiled when I read this one: "And all the people came early in the morning to hear [Jesus] at the temple" (Luke 21:38). I wrote in the margin of my Bible, "Can I get up early to hear Jesus?"

My adventure in prayer had begun. Soon the Lord would begin to show me the meaning of "listening prayer."

CHAPTER 5

Adventures in
Listening Prayer

*S*everal weeks after I began to rise early to pray, the Lord seemed to lay out five words that spoke to me about my prayer life. These five words came as I was praying. That was the beginning of *listening prayer.* (Listening prayer is discussed extensively in part 3 of this book.) I've meditated often on these five little words, and they have taken me to a deeper level of prayer.

THE 5 *D*s OF PRAYER

Desire. The first word the Lord whispered to my heart was *desire.* He helped me to see that *he* was giving me this desire to pray. If you have any desire to pray—no matter how small—it's from him! That's encouraging.

Recognize that desire and capture it to make it your own. I asked the Lord to intensify my desire for prayer. You can do the same thing. Believe me, he will take you up on it.

Decision. The second word the Lord brought to my mind

was *decision.* The Lord made it clear that I had come to a cross-roads in my spiritual journey. Either I was going to continue to pray daily, or I was going to go back to my haphazard way of praying.

The Lord seemed to be drawing a line in the sand. When I jotted down the date September 5, 1986, in my journal that first morning, I recognized that the Lord had helped me step across the line to pray. I have kept that date not only in my journal, but in my heart as well. It serves as a reminder of my decision and commitment.

I have noticed, whenever reading about men and women of prayer, that they all had a moment of decision when they committed to pray. S. D. Gordon said,

> The great people of the earth today are the people who pray. I do not mean those who talk about prayer; nor those who say they believe in prayer; nor yet those who can explain about *prayer*; but I mean those people who take *time* and *pray.* They have not time. It must be taken from some-thing else. This something else is important. Very impor-tant, and pressing, but still less important and less pressing than prayer.[5]

To pray is a choice and it requires a decision.

Discipline. The third word that the Lord impressed on me was a difficult but very necessary one: *discipline.* I discovered that prayer takes a place and a time. Of course, I often pray while I drive or while I walk. Prayer-walking around your neigh-borhood is a wonderful way to begin to reach your neighbors for Christ. However, there is something very important about having a time of prayer without extra distractions.

I realize that a popular approach to prayer is called "pray as you go." If you can't spend time in a "secret place," some advise, then just pray while you are doing your normal activities. This may be a low-guilt approach, but I wonder why we are afraid to challenge people to spend dedicated time with the Lord. Praying as you go is good, but it is not enough.

I'm sure Jesus used the pray–as-you-go method, but I know he also valued spending time in prayer in a secluded spot, free from external distractions. While you might try to get by on short conversations with your spouse or a close friend, it's the long, intimate conversations that truly bind you to someone. What is a marriage or a close friendship without deliberate, extended conversation? Intimacy requires intentional development.

As a young mom, time was a very precious commodity. (It still is.) It probably is for you too. For me, time proved to be the biggest hurdle to jump on the rigorous track of discipline.

I know a nurse who has been trained to end each patient examination by making two statements. First she asks, "Do you have any questions?" She then adds, "I have time for you." That is exactly what we are saying to the Lord when we enter this prayer commitment: *Father, I have time for you, your Word, and prayer. I'm staying in this spot until I say all that I need to say and you share all that you want to tell me.*

And, hard as it is, discipline was my training ground for listening in prayer. Yes, some days I was tired and discouraged. Other times I wondered if God was even listening. However, the Lord seemed to send just enough answers to prayer—and allowed just enough problems—to keep me coming back to him.

I've borrowed a popular phrase from business and time management experts to help keep me on track: First things first. Meeting with the Lord is a "first thing." When I'm tempted to do something else first—like check e-mail or read the paper—this phrase often seems to pop into my mind and keep me disciplined.

Interestingly, it was my daily disciplined time with God's

Word that brought me to a place of deep affection for Jesus Christ. It was then this affection for Jesus that brought me back to a place of prayer each morning. It turned into what I call a "victorious cycle."

Delight. When I sensed the fourth word was *delight,* I wondered if that was truly possible. Thankfully, I discovered that discipline will always give way to delight. After meeting with the Lord for several months, it became easier to get out of bed. I truly began to enjoy God. I started anticipating my time with him with hope and expectation. Time with the Lord *does* become delightful. I can honestly say now, nineteen years later, that I am actually eager to meet with the Lord in the morning. I can hardly wait to talk *and* listen to him.

"Taste and see that the Lord is good" (Psalm 34:8) has become meaningful to me. I "tasted" the Lord and found him to be good; I wanted to have more of him. When my children were young, I used to buy natural peanut butter because I was told it was better for them. But once a neighbor offered them *regular* peanut butter, I could not get our kids to go back to natural peanut butter. Once they tasted the new kind, they wanted it again and again.

The same is true for tasting the Lord. You go back to your place of prayer because you enjoy it! No longer is it a duty but a wonderful privilege. I believe something else happens as you get to this point in your friendship with the Lord: you begin to think about him more. All of a sudden your place of prayer is not only in your quiet spot each day—you also find yourself talking to him throughout your day, wherever you are and whatever you are doing. This is what the Bible calls praying without ceasing (1 Thessalonians 5:17, NKJV). In this stage of delight you are more aware of the Lord's involvement in your day. You recognize his presence when others around you may not see it. Your thoughts turn to God more quickly than they did before. In this stage, you *crave* more of God.

When you are in the discipline stage you have devotion time because you *have to* be with God. In the delight stage, you have devotion time because you *want to* be with God. There is a big difference! The Lord never intended our time with him to be a burden for us. It is never a duty for him to meet with us—we are in a relationship with him.

> *Keep on praying. No matter what happens, always be thankful.*
>
> **1 Thessalonians 5:17-18,** NLT

As a mom, I feel delight when one of my children sets out to please me. One day, just before leaving the house, I noticed that the clean, unfolded laundry had piled up to Mount Everest–size proportions. Normally, I ask each child to take a turn folding clothes. This particular day, however, I had not assigned the chore to anyone. I dreaded the thought of returning to this "mountain view" later in the day.

When I returned home later that afternoon, I could not believe my eyes. Every single piece of laundry for our family of seven had been neatly folded! Our daughter, Holly, a high schooler at the time, had seen the pile of unfolded clothes. No one forced her to fold those clothes—or even asked her to. I was thankful that the laundry was folded, but I was even more overjoyed by her heart's motivation. Holly had anticipated a need of my mine and met it out of love. She delighted to demonstrate her love for me.

Likewise, how pleased God must be when we willingly commit time to pray. God could demand us to help him in the work of prayer, but he doesn't. He waits to see if we will notice the amount of prayer that needs to be done, and, out of love for him, pick it up and continue praying until the job is done. Epaphras, the "prayer wrestler," is an example of perseverance in prayer. Paul writes that Epaphras is "always wrestling in prayer for you." He prayed that the believers in Colossae would "stand firm in all the will of God, mature and fully assured"

(Colossians 4:12). That wouldn't happen overnight. Epaphras was committed to praying over the long run for their spiritual growth. I love a phrase I came across in the writings of old prayer warriors: They admonished their readers to "pray through"—in other words, pray until God reveals his answer.

Holly didn't say, "I'll just fold the clothes for ten minutes and then stop." She stayed until the job was done. That is how I believe the Lord wants us to pray—not just for ten minutes or even for an hour—but until the job is done. There *is* a difference between duty and delight.

If your time of prayer is burdensome, you may need to reevaluate it. Perhaps you've just begun the discipline of praying and you are already discouraged. Or you tried praying for a few weeks, but now you have given up. May I encourage you to begin again? Remember, your enemy Satan does not want you to pray. He will seek to discourage you however he can. But don't underestimate the Resurrection power of Jesus Christ. His desire is for you to pray and to come alongside you to help you. Some days you may have to keep going to your place of prayer even though you don't feel like it. It took months for me to really want to meet with the Lord. But now I could not live without this time.

Perhaps it is like beginning an exercise program. Our daughter Abby never looked forward to the two-week conditioning program she was required to go through each spring for soccer. She and her teammates had to run and run. Just when she thought she could stop she was pushed to run more. Her whole body ached! She would even ask herself why she had signed up for soccer. She knew, however, that at their first game the grueling discipline would pay off. The team was in shape to run, and game day was much easier.

Daily. The final *D* the Lord put on my heart was *daily*. I realized that I needed to spend time with him every day, not just when I felt like it. When I mentioned this to a friend, she told me she was concerned that I would become legalistic. Her remark surprised and bothered me.

The Pharisees, the religious leaders of Jesus' day, set aside several times a day for prayer. For many of them, it was simply a legalistic ritual, and their time with God did nothing for them or for God. They spent time learning the Scriptures but many times missed the Author of those Scriptures. I did not want that kind of time alone with God, so I almost allowed my friend's words to sway me.

After praying about it, however, I came to these conclusions: that I *do* need to spend daily time with the Lord and that Jesus feels the loss of our devotion time more than we do. After all, in the Garden of Gethsemane, Jesus didn't really ask his disciples to do anything except keep him company. Three times he came to them hoping for their company, only to find them sleeping (Matthew 26:36-46). James Houston says, "Prayer is keeping company with God."[6]

In addition, I learned that there was no way for me to know God's agenda for the day unless I took the time to talk to him about it. Jesus himself needed time alone with his Father, and if *he* needed that, how much more do I? Scripture says that Jesus, on the night before he died, went out "as usual" to the Mount of Olives to pray (Luke 22:39). "As usual" implies that prayer was a normal, daily practice for him. Jesus always followed his Father's agenda.

In fact, Jesus' earthly life revolved around daily prayer. It is interesting to note that Jesus was praying as he was baptized (Luke 3:21). He was also listening to his Father at the same time. We are privileged that Scripture records his Father's words: "You are my beloved Son, and I am fully pleased with you" (Luke 3:22, NLT).

Jesus also prayed as he was transfigured before his disciples (Luke 9:29). Luke recorded God's words to his Son: "This is my Son, whom I have chosen; listen to him" (Luke 9:35). Many times the Bible tells us that Jesus prayed before healing some-one. He did not pray because it was a duty to perform; rather, through prayer he maintained his intimate relationship with his Father. It was his *usual* practice.

Whenever Jesus came back from praying he was fueled up. His time with his Father did not weigh him down; it buoyed him up. Interestingly, Jesus did not stop praying when he returned to heaven. Hebrews 7:25 communicates that Jesus always lives to intercede for us.

Think of that! Jesus is praying for you daily, and only he knows how many times a day he prays for you. Psalm 68:19 says: "Praise be to the Lord, to God our Savior, who *daily* bears our burdens." Since Jesus is daily bearing our burdens, we need to daily give our burdens to him.

Have you ever had anyone say to you, "I'm praying for you every day"? How did that make you feel? Are you able to genu-inely say to someone, "I'm praying for you daily"? What a tremendous gift we bestow on others when we intercede for them on a daily basis. You will never be more like Jesus Christ than when you are interceding for others.

Currently 139 women from our church pray for our family and ministry. We call them our "Lydia Ladies." (Lydia is men-tioned in Acts 16.) Another 99 men are on the pastor's prayer support team. These men and women are committed pray-ers and intercessors! Often on Sundays they tell me, "I pray for you and your family every day." Some get up at 5 A.M. to pray for us. These faithful prayer warriors even set their alarm for 2 A.M. to pray for my husband and me when we spoke in another time zone. We could not do ministry without their daily intercession.

A DAY AT THE WHITE HOUSE

I often think that if we truly understood what it means to enter the throne room of God, we would make prayer a much higher priority. Last year, I gained a fresh perspective on this.

In April a woman named Lindsey left a message for us on our answering machine. She said she was calling from the White House. At first we thought it was a joke.

We returned the call anyway and discovered that she really did work for the president. She invited my husband and me to a reception with President and Mrs. Bush at the White House for the upcoming National Day of Prayer.

Paul and I were shocked! An appointment at the White House! We made that visit a priority and dropped everything else that was scheduled that day.

When we arrived at the White House on May 2, we had to wait with seventy other guests for our turn to go through a security checkpoint and a metal detector. We were told that a background security check had been done on all the invited guests prior to our arrival.

Guides greeted us as we entered the building. In the lobby, a military orchestra played classical music. As our hosts led us to the dining room in the East Wing, we passed portraits of past presidents on the walls. Once we reached the dining room, another surprise awaited us. Instead of the cookies and punch I expected, long tables, covered with linen and decorated with fresh floral arrangements, were loaded with appetizers, sliced roast beef, carved turkey, shrimp, and many delicate desserts.

After filling our plates, we wandered into the Red Room and sat down to eat. As I ate, I thought of the correlations between the invitation from the White House and the invitation the Lord extends to us. As much of an honor as it was to see the president of the United States, we have the greater privilege of meeting with the King of kings every day! Unlike a visit to the president, which is preceded by time-consuming security measures, we are told to come boldly to the throne of heaven (Hebrews 4:16).

And while the array of food was amazing at the White House, it cannot compare to God's banqueting table. We can "feast" with the Lord each day on earth, and one day he will take us to the glorious marriage supper of the Lamb!

After we ate, we were led into the State Room where President and Mrs. Bush addressed each of us. As the White House reception wound down, we began to walk slowly to the exit. No one was in a hurry to go. In fact, the guides began to gently encourage us to do so. I was in the last group of people to leave. We took a few pictures outside the White House and walked back to our hotel. Our visit was over.

How grateful I am that the Lord never encourages us to leave his presence. He extends an open-door invitation that never limits our access to the King of kings and Lord of lords. What other king or president invites us to eat with him each day?

THE CYCLE CONTINUES

I find that the five words that the Lord impressed on me as I began my journey of prayer—desire, decision, discipline, delight, and daily—continue to challenge me. For instance, several times I have asked the Lord to increase my desire to pray. Desire is not just a wish; it is a deep craving for God. Desire must always come before prayer because it draws us deeper into our praying.

Deciding to begin praying was one of the best decisions I have ever made. (I think that fear of failure kept me from making that decision sooner.) Although I made that initial decision years ago, it is still a choice I must make and act upon every day with the Lord's help.

I have been challenged not just to set a daily appointment with God, but to keep it. Often Paul and I will say to someone, "We'd really like to get together with you sometime." Unless we get a date down on the calendar, however, it doesn't happen despite our good intentions. I now keep my prayer appointments as I would appointments with my doctor.

Being disciplined in prayer has affected me in a way I never dreamed possible. I'm basically a messy person. (If you peeked into my kitchen cabinets or laundry room, you'd have to agree!) So much of my life used to be really disorganized and undisciplined. However, having this one area of disciplined prayer has affected many other areas of my life. Discipline has pleasant boundaries that have helped me feel safe and prepared for whatever comes into my day.

Scripture tells us to "take delight in the Lord, and he will give you your heart's desires" (Psalm 37: 4, NLT). I have taken God up on this promise and have seen over and over how seeking the Lord brings a true, fulfilling delight, as well as assurance of his boundless love.

Take a moment and check your spiritual pulse. Which word—desire, decision, discipline, delight, or daily—best describes where God may be working to enrich your prayer life right now?

CHAPTER 6

Finding God in Prayer

*J*oni Eareckson Tada writes about "God's best friends" in her devotional *Diamonds in the Dust.*[7]

I like that phrase, though I realize at first it may sound strange. Joni is not saying that God has favorites. Rather, "God's best friends" are those who have made God *their* best friend. One of the reasons for that close relationship is the regular time they spend with him in prayer.

As appealing as it may be to think of ourselves as "God's best friends," a life of prayer is not easy. No matter how much you desire to pray and listen, you'll face hindrances. Satan is behind many of them. Remember Jesus' disciple Simon Peter? Jesus told him, "Simon, Simon, Satan has asked to have all of you, to sift you like wheat. But I have pleaded in prayer for you, Simon, that your faith should not fail" (Luke 22:31-32, NLT). Clearly Satan wanted to hinder God's kingdom—after all, Peter was to be a key person in building the church of Jesus Christ.

Much later in life, Peter understood Satan's evil intentions. He wrote, "Your enemy the devil prowls around like a roaring lion looking for someone to devour" (1 Peter 5:8). Peter understood that Satan is bent on our demise. He does not want us to pray or to call on the mighty, powerful name of Jesus. The devil knows that will be *his* demise! We can be assured that he will never prompt us to pray. He knows that when we do, we push back his kingdom and advance God's. He knows that our prayers can actually undo years of his work. It is no wonder that our enemy will try to stop us from praying. If there were no devil, there would be no difficulty in praying. This privilege called prayer is serious work!

THE PRAYER TRAPS

"There is no limit to what any Christian may accomplish through prayer," said author and former missionary Wesley Duewel.[8] Satan knows this, and he is the "master distracter" who seeks to encourage our naturally selfish tendencies and discourage us from prayer. If he can get us to overestimate our own abilities and underestimate the power of prayer, our prayer life will fall flat. Here are seven harmful attitudes or traps that can stall our prayer life before it starts:

Trap 1: "Prayer doesn't make that much of a difference." Satan does not want us to grasp the importance of prayer. He too is familiar with the Scripture, "You do not have, because you do not ask God" (James 4:2). He hopes you'll think that your prayers don't matter so you won't bother to ask.

He knows that if we understand the significance of prayer, we will be desperate for God—desperate to rely on him for everything. You've heard the old saying, "God won't give you any more than you can handle." My friend Pam Chun likes to say, "God always gives us *more* than we can handle. If we could handle it by ourselves, we wouldn't need or seek God."

Trap 2: "I'm too busy to pray!" Though busyness often seems like a by-product of modern life, Scripture has a lot to say about this trap. Remember the response of the two sisters Mary and Martha when Jesus visited their home? Martha hustled anxiously about in the kitchen preparing a meal while Mary sat attentively at Jesus' feet.

I'm so glad Martha's conversation with Jesus is recorded in Luke 10:40-42. When she complained about having to do all the work, Jesus gently chided her: "Martha, Martha, you are worried and upset about many things, but only one thing is needed. Mary has chosen what is better, and it will not be taken away from her." True, Martha was busy doing work for the Lord, but she was distracted, worried, and upset.

Do you ever get that way while doing ministry? Do you spend much of your life feeling rushed and harried? Have you ever felt guilty because you *weren't* busy? When someone else tells you how busy she is, do you sometimes find yourself trying to "top" her story with your own? If you're like most people, the answer is yes.

Busyness is the way of life for most of us. Ironically, it is precisely at our busiest times that we most need to pray. When the Holy Spirit finds a "busy signal" in my heart, I know it is my wake-up call to stop and reevaluate my schedule. I may have to "plan to neglect" some things of lesser priority.

Don't fall into the trap of being so busy *for* God that you forget to spend time *with* him. Someone once noted that "God has many servants but few friends." Jesus made it clear that he wants to be our friend. "No longer do I call you servants, for a servant does not know what his master is doing; but I have called you friends, for all things that I heard from My Father I have made known to you" (John 15:15, NKJV). How much easier it is to *do* something for God than to cultivate a friendship with him!

So often we make ministry more important than prayer. The proper order, however, is prayer, obedience, then ministry.

Trap 3: "God hasn't answered, so I might as well quit praying."
Satan wants us to stop praying before we should. Persevere in
prayer! Don't give up; keep on asking. Two of the Bible's para-
bles on prayer address the importance of perseverance (Luke
11:5-10 and Luke 18:1-8). The story of the persistent neighbor
who asks for food at midnight and the parable of a widow who
repeatedly appeals for justice from an evil judge show that even
humans usually respond to repeated pleas for help. How much
more does God long to bless us when we repeatedly bring our
requests to him!

I use the acronym PUSH—Pray Until Something Happens.
Last year my friend Peggy asked another woman and me to
meet with her for prayer. Peggy needed professional counseling
but was afraid to go. Even if she had the boldness to go, she did
not know how she could afford the counseling sessions.

The three of us prayed that the Lord would give Peggy courage to get the help she needed. We also prayed that God would
provide for her financial need. We thought the Lord would
answer our prayers right away. Month after month passed as the
three of us cried out to the Lord with much prayer and fasting.
There was only silence from heaven and no breakthrough for my
friend Peggy. I was tempted many times to try to make things
happen, but I sensed that I needed to wait for the Lord to act.

Finally, eleven months after the first time we prayed with
Peggy, God revealed his plan. The Lord not only gave her the
courage to begin counseling, he also provided a godly counselor
and someone to make the payments. By waiting, she had access
to the best counselor, as well as freedom from financial burden.

Looking back, we now see the process that the Lord was
silently taking us on. "Your path led through the sea, your way
through the mighty waters, though your footprints were not seen"
(Psalm 77:19). While we could not "see" God working, he deep-
ened our dependency on him. His timing and purposes were perfect.

Our culture elevates independence. But God asks us to stop

trying to work things out in our own way and depend on him and his timing. Scripture says he is "able to do far more than we would ever dare to ask or even dream of" (Ephesians 3:20, TLB). I am learning the truth of God's Word when he whispers, "In the time of my favor I will answer you" (Isaiah 49:8).

Jesus told his disciples a story to illustrate their need for constant prayer and to show them that they must never give up.

Luke 18:1, NLT

Trap 4: "I just forget to pray about things." We have not because we ask not (James 4:2). Sometimes prayer is our last resort instead of our first idea.

At times I find myself in what seems an impossible situation when I remember I have not prayed about it. The Lord invites us to pray about *everything.* Nothing is too small or too big for him. I'm sure God shakes his head sadly when we do not ask for his guidance, for he knows exactly how to help us. My husband and I are honored when our married kids call and say, "Mom and Dad, can you please give us some financial counsel?" or "What do you think about us going overseas for an entire summer to work with a church plant?" We do not resent them asking, and neither does God resent us asking him. In fact, he waits for us to come to him.

I came across a story in Corrie ten Boom's writings that reminded me to always go to God first when I have a need. While Corrie was in solitary confinement at a Nazi concentration camp, she learned that her father had died. Corrie cried out to a passing guard, "This letter just came—it says that my father has died."

The guard responded with a "so what" type of answer and walked away. Corrie, who was naturally hurting and looking for consolation, suddenly stopped and cried out to God. "Dear Jesus, how foolish of me to have called for human help when You are here."[9]

I too needed to learn to go to God first in any situation. If he wants to use other people to help me, he will either bring them to me or lead me to them.

Trap 5: "Why pray when complaining feels so good?" A friend told me not long ago that one reason she failed to ask God for help was because she *liked* dwelling on her problem. It made her feel more in control when she could stay fixed on the problem.

Criticism and complaining will quench your prayer life and the Holy Spirit's voice. You will never hear a critical or pessimistic word from God! There is no darkness in him at all. Jesus Christ is our defender who protects us against our accusing, negative enemy. I am learning that I must shift from pouting to praise, and it takes a conscious choice on my part.

I had identical twin aunts named Hortence and Harriet who were extremely difficult to tell apart. They had similar tastes and even shopped alike. One could go downtown in the morning to buy a dress, and the other would shop in the afternoon. They would find out later that they had bought the same dress.

Although their looks and tastes were identical, their temperaments were just the opposite. As a child, all I had to do was wait for one to talk to know which aunt was speaking. One aunt was positive and affirming. The other aunt was negative and critical.

One night as I helped my critical aunt dry the dishes, I unknowingly left some water on the bottom of a pan. The next thing I knew she was wiping the wet pan across my cheek. "Do you feel that?" she yelled. "You didn't dry the bottom of this pan." I'm sure you can guess which aunt I always chose to be around! My critical aunt quenched our relationship; I never did get to know her.

Philippians 2:14 instructs us to "do everything without complaining." When we fall into the trap of complaining and being critical, we do not please the Lord. This negative thinking can quench the Holy Spirit's dynamic presence in our life. I believe Satan loves it when we criticize others. I also believe it saddens the Holy Spirit. He would prefer we pray for them.

Trap 6: "My sin isn't that big of a deal." Scripture makes it clear that sin is an obvious roadblock to prayer. "If I had not confessed the sin in my heart, my Lord would not have listened" (Psalm 66:18, NLT).

Some people harbor a sin or harmful habit but have decided not to do anything about it. They justify a quick peek at a porno-graphic Web site, for instance, rationalizing that it's okay since it's done in the privacy of their home—and they buy into the lie that it might even add a little excitement to their marriage. The end result of willful sin is a stunted prayer life.

Thankfully, confession and repentance can free us from this snare. (Sometimes, as with an addiction to pornography, professional counseling is needed to help strugglers reach this point.) People often quote this familiar verse from James: "The prayer of a righteous man is powerful and effective." Yet many times, the first part of that verse is omitted: "Therefore confess your sins to each other and pray for each other so that you may be healed" (James 5:16). If we want prayers to be a powerful and effective force in our lives, we must repent of our sins.

Trap 7: "I want God to do things my way!" When we do pray, Satan wants to trip us up so that we pray with wrong motives. This morning I read Mark 10:35-37, where Jesus' disciples came to him and said, "Teacher . . . we want you to do for us what-ever *we* ask" (italics mine).

Although Jesus knew what was in their hearts, he graciously responded, "What do you want me to do for you?"

James and John replied, "Let one of us sit at your right and the other at your left in your glory." James and John were moti-vated by a desire for powerful places of position.

It's easy for us to pray with wrong motives too. *Lord, let me get that promotion at work because I think I am better qualified than my coworker who is up for the same position.* It is easy to pray amiss by having the same mind-set as James and John— "We want you to do for us whatever *we* ask."

To pray correctly is to say: *Father, you know the desire of my heart about that position, but above all I want what you want for me; I want your will.* When we pray, *Your will be done,* it is never a cop-out. It was and continues to be the way Jesus prays. He always wants what his Father wants.

DIVINE DELIVERANCE

In addition to laying traps, Satan tries to trip us up in other ways. When an unexpected curve enters our day, all thoughts of God and his Resurrection power drain out of us. For example, I can be enjoying my day, rejoicing in God's mercies—until someone calls and complains about something. Instantly I dwell on that comment and no longer think about God's goodness.

There is good news, however. When Satan throws what I call his "daggers of *D*s"—discouragement, distraction, dismay, and depression—the Lord offers a beautiful *D* word to cover every wound the enemy inflicts: deliverance. (I am not talking about clinical, prolonged depression here. I am simply referring to those days when things just don't go right.)

As you learn to train your thoughts to dwell on the Lord Jesus every day, you will find yourself refocusing on God more quickly. I try to use every "dagger" that comes along as a reminder to pray. The moment my spirit goes down, I take it as a signal for me to talk to the Lord and praise him as well.

Something interesting happens as we talk to him more about what is going on in our day: we begin to listen more. We develop a "life of prayer" or a "prayer lifestyle."

BEGINNING YOUR JOURNEY OF PRAYER

Above all, don't allow negative thinking or Satan's ploys to keep you from prayer. The only way to learn to pray is simply to do it. Pray, pray, pray! Appendix B, "A Prayer Test," offers you a way to quickly evaluate your present prayer life, in what may be an eye-opening exercise.

Ultimately, it doesn't matter how you structure your time with God; it is just important that you set a time and meet with him. I believe the Lord will help you tailor your time with him in a way that is unique to you.

I describe the way God and I meet, therefore, not to suggest that it is *the* way to spend time in the Bible and prayer but

> *Jesus went out to a mountainside to pray, and spent the night praying to God.*
>
> **Luke 6:12**

simply that it is one way. I spend my quiet time in a walk-in closet in our bedroom. I read a devotional to help me get started. Next I read the Bible until God speaks to my heart. I then journal that Scripture. This is also when I pray for others. I close my quiet time in silence, listening as I sit still.

While the time and place for meeting with God varies from person to person, I highly recommend that you find someone to help keep you accountable in meeting with God. An account-ability friend should be someone who is in the Word, faithful in prayer, and not afraid to ask the hard questions in life. Such a person can say with the apostle Paul, "Follow my example, as I follow the example of Christ" (1 Corinthians 11:1).

I meet with three trusted friends for breakfast and prayer once a month. "What do you see God doing in your life right now?" and "How can we pray for you?" are questions that we ask one another each time we meet.

I also have a mentor and friend, Kathleen, who is completely in love with Jesus. She spends hours interceding for people. Her God-given compassion motivates her to pray for others. She also helps keep me accountable in my spiritual journey. If you don't have someone like this in your life, ask the Lord to send a person of his choosing to come alongside you. I prayed many years for a "Kathleen" in my life, and she was worth the wait.

TALKING TO A FRIEND

Remember that the Holy Spirit himself cheers you on as you launch into prayer. He is the best mentor and accountability friend there is, and he will help you as you begin your daily prayer time. You may not be sure how to start, so let me share some suggestions:

Talk with God like you would a friend. Don't worry about how to word your prayers. Pray conversationally. Leave some gaps between your sentences in case the Lord desires to speak to your heart as you are praying. Remember, prayer is two-way conversation.

Tell him your specific needs. We are invited to pray about *everything* (Philippians 4:6). God does not resent your asking him for help. You are never a burden or an inconvenience to him.

To keep you on track, you may want to keep a prayer-request list. I keep a small flat notebook in my Bible so that I can write down any requests. When someone asks me to pray for him or her, I write down the person's name, the request, and the date. Normally, I pray over those requests once a week. However, on other days, I look over the list and ask the Lord to bring to my attention the ones that he would like me to pray for that day. I am not enslaved to my prayer list, but I do find it very helpful in keeping me focused. It also serves as a good reminder to follow up with people I have promised to pray for.

My current prayer request notebook dates back to 1996. Each time the Lord answers one of my requests, I cross it off and write "Praise the Lord" next to it. I am astounded to see so many answers to prayer! Seeing how he has provided in the past helps me trust him with my future.

Ask him to point out anything in your life that needs correction. Many times I pray, *Lord, help hold me still long enough so that you* can *search me and know my heart* (Psalm 139:23). I once had to pass through a metal detector before entering an event attended by then-president Clinton. One of the detectors buzzed as I passed through. I couldn't figure out what was setting it off—I did not have my watch on, and there was no change in my pocket. Finally, the security guard asked if I had a foil gum wrapper in my pocket. I did. That little piece of foil was picked up by the very sensitive machine. The Holy Spirit functions the same way in our lives. He is very sensitive in detecting anything that will keep us from the Lord Jesus.

In Psalm 19:12, David says, "How can I know all the sins lurking in my heart? Cleanse me from these hidden faults" (NLT). Just last month I was telling the Lord that someone was being very critical. Quietly the Lord said to me, *How about you?* It took me by surprise. I had not realized I was in a negative, judgmental mode. Ouch! This fault was hidden to me but known to the Lord.

Try using the "ACTS" or "PRAY" acronyms for guided prayer. Many people follow these acronyms while praying. ACTS stands for: *A*—Adoration of the Lord; *C*—Confession of sin; *T*—Thanksgiving for all the Lord has done; *S*—Supplications made to the Lord on behalf of others. The other acronym, PRAY, is similar and is also helpful: *P*—Praise the Lord for what he is doing; *R*—Repent of sins; *A*—Ask the Lord for help with requests; *Y*—Yield to God and be still before him.

Praying ACTS has become very valuable to me. Sometimes I find myself omitting one of those letters, which can be very revealing. For instance, if I omit adoration, it means I have forgotten whom I am speaking to—the glorious One. If I omit confession, I either have some fear of revealing my guilt or perhaps a low view of God (thinking that he will overlook some "small" sin). If I omit thanksgiving, then I am not purposefully noticing all that God is doing around me. And if I am lacking in supplication, then I have lost my compassion for others and my desire that they come to know Jesus as Savior.

One helpful way to get started in guided prayer is to divide a spiral notebook into four sections, one for each type of prayer. You can then jot down requests or praises that correspond with each, adding notes as you see God respond to your requests.

Pray Scripture verses for your family members and others. You can use your Bible as a prayer book. Philippians 1:9-11 reads, "And this is my prayer: that your love may abound more and more in knowledge and depth of insight, so that you may be able to discern what is best and may be pure and blameless until the day of Christ, filled with the fruit of righteousness that comes through Jesus Christ—to the glory and praise of God." In the margin of my Bible next to that verse I wrote, "A prayer for our children."

Also, allow Scripture to help formulate your prayers. Recently I ran into a friend at the grocery store. She asked if I could give a verbal recommendation for a person she was thinking of hiring. I hesitated a bit. At first, I wanted to make ungraceful statements. The person had hurt several families with his words and actions.

I knew I needed to be guarded with my answer. It would have been dishonest to give a glowing report, but I also wanted the balance of "truth and grace" without any form of gossip. I swallowed hard and asked the Lord for wisdom. A verse I had just read that morning became my silent prayer: "The heart of the righteous weighs its answers, but the mouth of the wicked gushes evil" (Proverbs 15:28).

Lord, I silently and quickly prayed, *my first impulse is to want to "gush evil." Help me to be righteous in this situation. Please help me to weigh my words before they are spoken, and do not let my lips gush any kind of evil.* How grateful I was that the Holy Spirit reminded me of that verse and then helped to form it into a prayer. I told her that I had some concerns but also encouraged her to check with some other people for their recommendations.

Ask God to help you find prayer partners. Even the apostle

Paul knew he needed prayer partners. Many times he asked for prayer: "Pray for me" (Ephesians 6:19, TLB); "Pray for us" (Colossians 4:3); and "Brothers, pray for us" (1 Thessalonians 5:25). My favorite such request is, "I urge you, brothers, by our Lord Jesus Christ and by the love of the Spirit, to join me in my struggle by praying to God for me" (Romans 15:30). Paul had problems just like we do. He welcomed and depended on the prayers of his partners.

These six steps helped me launch into a regular time of prayer in my bedroom closet. But as I experienced the pleasure of talking with him there, I desired more. Once I had established my appointments with God in the morning, I realized that my time of prayer did not have to end there. It could continue throughout my entire day.

CHAPTER 7

Bringing Prayer out of the Closet

*A*uthor Randy Alcorn wrote that Satan's demons *"prey* without ceasing."[10]

That play on words caught my attention. If the demons *prey* on us relentlessly, then I need to *pray* to the Lord without ceasing. I want to be more persevering than they are. I need to be on guard for the arrows Satan shoots at me each day. I think we would be amazed if we had the eyes to see all the spiritual warfare that is going on around us. The devil is our relentless enemy. He tries to discourage, distract, defeat, and depress us in any way possible.

Once I thought praying unceasingly was not possible. Yet, at the same time I wondered why the Bible told us to "pray without ceasing" (1 Thessalonians 5:17, NKJV) if we were not able to do it. There had to be a way. I am finding that to pray unceasingly means to be ready to pray at any moment of the day, no matter what I am doing.

Today I pray—and listen for God's voice—not only in my prayer closet, but throughout my day. You can too.

GOOD MORNING, LORD

Listening for God can be the first thing you do each day. As soon as you open your eyes in the morning, train yourself to think about the Lord. Picture him standing at your bedside. Recognize his presence. This is a time to consciously reestablish your awareness of the partnership you have with almighty God. Ask that you would be *preoccupied with Christ* throughout your day.

Think of one thing for which you can praise and thank the Lord. It could be as simple as thanking him for helping you get out of bed today. This morning I was feeling a bit melancholy. I was in no mood to praise the Lord. I was in the midst of preparing for a speaking engagement, handling various phone calls, and trying to encourage a friend. I finally dropped everything and ran upstairs to lie facedown in my prayer closet *again* and cry out to the Lord.

I am so glad that he never tires of my coming to him! My heart was lifted as I, at first, *forced* myself to think of things to praise him for. That opened the door for praise to flow naturally, and I found healing. Praise and thanksgiving are great ways to help refocus our heart and thoughts. Praise makes a wonderful pathway through my doom-and-gloom thoughts straight to Jesus. It also helps me become "God-aware" during my day.

Ask the Lord to remind you to pray throughout your day. He will help you! One of the roles of the Holy Spirit is to remind us what he has taught us. Jesus says in John 14:26 that "the Counselor, the Holy Spirit, whom the Father will send in my name, will teach you all things and will *remind you of everything I have said to you*" (emphasis mine).

ALL IN THE FAMILY

I begin praying for my family early each day. In fact, if you are married, I encourage you to pray with your spouse. This is difficult for so many couples. That is why I advise engaged couples to start praying together now. The longer you wait, the harder it gets.

You and your spouse are your own unique prayer team. You are prayer partners for each other! The Lord says that when two or three are together, he is in the middle (Matthew 18:20). Connecting and bonding take place as you pray together. When I hear my husband pray, many times I pick up on things that I did not know he was dealing with. Listening to him pray for me endears him to me, plus it helps me know better how to pray for him.

> *Pray at all times and on every occasion in the power of the Holy Spirit. Stay alert and be persistent in your prayers for all Christians everywhere.*
> **Ephesians 6:18,** NLT

William Law, an eighteenth-century author and preacher, said, "There is nothing that makes us love someone so much as praying for them."[11] Satan knows about the powerful union that takes place when couples pray. Don't let him rob you of that closeness with God and each other. Take advantage of the times you are together during your day to pray: mealtimes, bedtime, walks together, and even during phone conversations. It doesn't have to be a regimented time, just do it.

Pray *with* and *for* your children or grandchildren throughout their day. Take advantage of the opportunities you have to model praying for them. When you pray with them, you might say, "Let's talk to Jesus" rather than, "Let's pray." It will help them understand that when we pray we are talking to a real person rather than going through a religious ritual.

Believe me, time teaching your children to pray will come back as a blessing to you. There are many times when my kids will now say to me, "Mom, let's pray about that together."

Author Richard Foster said, "If we truly love people, we will desire for them far more than it is within our power to give them, and this will lead us to prayer. Intercession is a way of loving others."[12]

It's true: you can love and influence your children through your prayers. I know a mom named Sharon who is an example of this. Her son decided to date a nonbeliever even though she and her husband had taught him early on about the importance of dating other believers. The more Sharon talked, the more her son wanted to date his non-Christian girlfriend.

Finally, Sharon decided to quit talking to her son and talk to the Lord instead. She began praying for this unsaved girl. A year later this young lady received Jesus as her Savior at her son's youth group. Sharon found out that this teen had no believers in her family and consequently no one had been praying for her to know Jesus. Eventually, this teen realized that her coming to know Jesus was a direct result of the Holy Spirit and Sharon's prayers.

Results from prayer are often the only way God's plan or purpose can be seen by an unbeliever. You cannot force others to love Jesus, but your prayers can release God's power to soften hearts. Sharon influenced this teen for Jesus through her earnest pleading with God.

By the way, you may be the only person praying for someone. Who prayed for *you* to come into the kingdom? Who are *your* prayers influencing right now? Prayer is the greatest work you can do on earth! Oswald Chambers said, "Praying is our holy occupation."[13]

I am challenged by this insight from E. M. Bounds: "Woe to the generation of sons who find their censers empty of the rich incense of prayer; whose fathers have been too busy or too unbelieving to pray, and perils inexpressible and consequences untold are their unhappy heritage. Fortunate are they whose fathers and mothers have left them a wealthy patrimony (estate) of prayer."[14]

OUT AND ABOUT

Pray as you drive, walk, exercise, or wait for someone. Ask the Lord to help this become second nature for you (or maybe first nature!).

Let your community landmarks remind you to pray. As you drive past schools, churches, or neighborhoods, pray for them.

Have you ever thought to pray for your server when you eat at a restaurant? Usually the waiter or waitress has a name tag, so you can pray silently for him or her by name.

Some friends told us that as they were bowing their head to pray at a restaurant, their waitress suddenly showed up. While some people would have found that situation awkward, they did not. One of our friends simply said to their server, "You know, we were just getting ready to pray. Is there anything we can pray about for *you?*" Instantly their waitress's eyes filled with tears and she rattled off a whole list of requests. Our friend then prayed right there in the restaurant for her.

These friends have seen God use this way of praying in powerful ways. You never know when your offer to pray for others will deeply touch them. (A note of caution: If your server sees you praying, make sure you treat him or her well and make Jesus look attractive. Our son-in-law Adam, who waited tables while going to seminary, said that sometimes Christians left him religious tracts *instead* of tips. He said this was a turnoff for the nonbelievers he worked with.)

MAKE A JOYFUL NOISE

Pray out loud when you can. I like to do this when I am alone in the car. It keeps me more focused. Many times I have people tell me that it is hard for them to pray in a small group. By praying out loud when you are alone, the Lord can help break down the barrier when praying with others.

Praise the Lord as much as you can during your day. My husband, Paul, taught me the method of "praise prayers." Years ago he challenged one of our small groups to pray our requests but to do it completely using praise and thanksgiving (no asking).

For example, someone might say: "Thank you, Father, that while Ted is going to have surgery on Tuesday, you will be in that surgery room with him. Thank you that you will be guiding the doctor's hands and giving him the skills that he needs. I praise you that you are the great Physician."

Not long ago I was praying with some friends over a heavy issue. We decided to pray for these weighty matters totally with praise. We came out of that prayer session with much lighter hearts and spirits.

My friend Mary uses nature to prompt her to praise the Lord. She asks him to let her see at least one of his "wonders" each day. Recently we had a huge winter storm that dumped about ten inches of lake-effect snow on us. Personally, I was not too excited about the snow and complained about it continually.

Mary called me during that time and exclaimed, "Marilyn, isn't the snow beautiful? Just look at how many inches of snow are on the ground."

Just when I was about ready to grumble back to her, she added, "Think of the vast number of individual snowflakes it took to build up all that snow—and every snowflake is different. Isn't God incredible?"

After she hung up I looked out our kitchen window. Instead of seeing the huge mounds of snow, I saw tiny, fragile, individual snowflakes all piled up in my backyard. Snowflakes designed by God! "Wow, God, you are amazing," I said. "Look at what your delicate little flakes can do when they all stick together." Praise changed my attitude.

Don't limit your praise to spoken words either! Sing your praise to the Lord throughout your day. I don't really want anyone to hear me sing, but it is fun to make up a song of praise and sing it while I am driving alone in the car. I have no idea where the melody will go or what my exact words will be, but it makes me think through my praise. This method of praying may sound strange, but two days ago I read in Psalm 47:6: "Sing praises to God, sing praises; sing praises to our King, sing praises." Wow, four times in one verse we are told to *sing* praise! Maybe it's not so strange!

SHORT BUT SWEET

Sometimes our time is limited or we are consumed in a project. That does not mean we cannot seek God's help or hear his voice. Pray quick "arrow" prayers throughout your day. When you have agreed to pray for someone, ask the Holy Spirit to bring that name to your remembrance whenever he desires. When he does, say a prayer on that person's behalf.

Learn the value of "flash" prayers. Anytime you are talking to someone, quickly and silently ask the Lord to help you know how best to respond to that person. Sometimes a person may ask for advice. Before you answer, send up an SOS flash to the Lord.

Pray "spot" prayers with people. If someone comes up to you and shares a problem, ask if you can pray with her right then. Most hurting people will not turn you down. Many times we find it easier to say, "I'll pray for you when I get home." Try praying on the spot. This is also helpful when someone asks for prayer but you cannot honestly promise to pray for him daily. In such cases, I pray with the person on the spot and then say, "As the Lord reminds me of this need, I will pray for you." I also have begun to pray "spot" prayers of thanksgiving with those who tell me how God has answered a request.

Two months ago at a women's retreat where I was speaking, a young mom told me that test results revealed that the baby she was carrying had cystic fibrosis. She had gotten the results right before leaving for the retreat. In fact, she had almost decided not to come because she was struggling with the difficult news.

We talked awhile and then prayed together. After we prayed, both of us were in tears. I embraced her and said I would write her name down and lift her and her baby in prayer to our heavenly Father as he reminded me to pray for her. The Lord is so faithful! Many times he prompted me to pray for her even though I did not say I would pray daily for her.

I just received a letter from her, now two months later. She wrote: "We've seen God answer our prayers about our baby. The amniocentesis confirmed he does not have cystic fibrosis; rather, they believe he has developed a small harmless mass of extra lung tissue."

Praise the Lord; he had done a wondrous thing! Because I took time to pray on the spot for this woman, I ended up being blessed as well. My faith was boosted as I learned how God had divinely intervened for this family.

I find it helpful to ask two questions of people with whom I pray on the spot. First I ask, "How are *you* praying about this situation?" Many times people will stop and reply, "That's a good question; I'm not sure." This often tells me that they want *me* to pray, but they themselves have not really prayed about the matter. It's important for them to pray about their own need as well.

The second question I ask is, "What are you asking God to do in this situation?" This causes the person to consider what *God's* purposes may be. His purposes and glory should be our highest goal in prayer.

Talking on the phone is another good time to say spot prayers with others. My husband is really good about remembering to do this. He will often say, "Would it be all right if I took a moment to pray for you?" The other day he called a family from our church who had lost a loved one. The family was not home so he prayed over the phone and left the message on their answering machine. They later shared how much that prayer blessed their hurting family members. They played that message over and over.

Praying over e-mail is also a meaningful gift. When I do this I begin by writing something like, "This is how I am praying for you today . . ." and then explain how I am lifting them up to the Lord.

FOCUSED PRAYERS

Have you ever felt helpless or frustrated as you watched the evening news or read your newspaper? There is something you can do. Lift up daily prayers for our leaders in government. Whether or not you agree with them, Scripture tells us to pray for those in authority (1 Timothy 2:2). This is not just a request, but a *command*. From police officers to the president of the United States—we are admonished to pray for our leaders.

While George W. Bush was running for the presidency in 2000, he campaigned in our state. One February evening my husband received a phone call at home saying that then-governor Bush would be campaigning in western Michigan that weekend. Would it be all right if he worshiped at our church with us? He did not want to seek votes at our church; in fact, he did not want to say a single word to the congregation. He just wanted to worship. My husband said that we would be honored to have him worship with us.

Sunday arrived and so did many politicians and dignitaries. I was seated in a pew waiting for the service to begin when suddenly Governor Bush was led to where I was sitting! I had expected him to sit with some of the elected officials from our state. I felt a bit flustered as he was seated between my husband and me. He quickly put me at ease as he smiled and said hello.

When my husband got up to pray, he prayed for Governor Bush, Laura, and their daughters. After Paul finished praying, Governor Bush whispered to me, "Please thank your husband for praying for my wife and daughters. That means so much to me."

I told him I would and then added, "Prayer is the best gift we can give to someone, isn't it?"

He smiled and said, "Yes, it really is."

A little later in the service I opened my Bible. There between the pages of my Bible was a verse printed on a small laminated card that my mentor, Kathleen, had given me. Governor Bush evidently saw it, because he leaned over to me and said, "I like that card."

"Oh, would you like to have it?" I asked.

When he said yes, I handed him the card. He thanked me and tucked it into his pocket. The verse? "But I trust in you, O Lord; I say, 'You are my God.' My times are in your hands" (Psalm 31:14-15).

I did not realize at the time how much that verse was going to apply to him after he was elected to the presidency later that year. I often wonder if the Lord has reminded him of that verse from the laminated card. I continue to pray that verse for him, and at times, all of Psalm 31. The Lord spoke to my heart loud and clear. I *must* be faithful to lift up our elected leaders in prayer.

We should not limit our prayers to our nation, however. Ask the Lord to give you a burden to pray for another country. I made it a matter of prayer to find out which country or countries the Lord would have me focus on. Our missionary friends have really influenced me in praying this way. Use daily TV news reports or newspapers to prompt you to pray for the country that God lays on your heart. Web sites from Christian ministries and humanitarian agencies can provide detailed information and specific prayer requests. Three I highly recommend are www.hcjb.org, www.opendoorsusa.org, and www.persecution.com.

Right now I feel led to pray for three particular countries. One of them is Hungary. My mother was born there, and while I have never visited the place of her birth, it has captured my heart. I know from our missionaries with HCJB World Radio that there is currently an urgent need for a Christian radio station in

Hungary. The permit has been turned down by the government several times. The ministry also needs to find someone living in Hungary to manage the station once it is established. Neither my mother nor her family members heard the gospel when they lived in Hungary, so I feel a special burden for this country.

The Lord is very specific about his command to go into all the nations to preach the gospel. I will most likely not go to all the nations, but I can go to them through the avenue of prayer. Jesus also gave us a very specific request to pray in this regard: "Ask [that means pray!] the Lord of the harvest, therefore, to send out workers into his harvest field" (Matthew 9:38). Our prayers advance the gospel!

Choose a country and ask the Lord to remind you to pray for it as you go about your day.

END AS YOU BEGAN

Let your final thoughts before you fall asleep at night rest on Jesus. Thank him for at least one thing he has done for you that day. The subconscious does not sleep, so this is an opportunity to invite the Holy Spirit to be present with you and your thoughts throughout the night. Invite him to wake you up in the night if he desires you to pray for someone. He will take you up on that invitation!

I have found that our minds are most open to God's editing in the middle of the night. I like how King Solomon described this loving attentiveness to our heavenly Father during the night hours: "I slept but my heart was awake" (Song of Songs 5:2).

From the time you awaken to the time you go to sleep, ask the Lord to train you to be more aware of his presence. Your prayer life will definitely be enlarged if you don't limit prayer to your "closet" but bring it with you into your day and night.

CHAPTER 8

When Praying Isn't Easy

*S*omething happened to me a couple of years after I began to be disciplined in prayer. I was going along, enjoying my time of sharing back and forth with my heavenly Father, when for some unknown reason, I could no longer "feel" God when I prayed.

I knew sin would hinder my prayers, so I searched my soul for weeks. *Lord, show me my sin, whatever it is. I want to experience the sweet fellowship I was experiencing before you turned silent. Why are you so quiet? What did I do, Father? Where did you go?*

Over and over I confessed every sin I knew about—even ones for which I had already asked forgiveness. I couldn't see God, and I couldn't feel God. It seemed as if he had abandoned me. I was depressed, figuring I must have displeased the Lord and made him angry with me.

My journals from that time describe my emotions. I felt as if I were driving a car through a very long, dark tunnel, feeling very alone. "I wonder where God is?" I wrote. I knew in my head God was there, but I kept asking him, "Why can't I *feel* you, Father? Why can't I 'see' you in this darkness?"

It took me months to understand what was happening. The Lord was teaching me, through prayer, to depend on him for who he is and not for how I feel about him. This time forced me to trust the Lord alone and not rely on my feelings.

Marilyn, you must learn to trust me for who you know I am according to my Word, God said to my heart. I discovered that God often speaks the loudest in his silence.

Although these times are spiritually enriching, I don't enjoy them one bit! The moment I realize I am heading into one of those dark tunnels, I groan, *Oh, Father, not again!*

SEEING IN THE DARK

Through this difficult period, I began to learn the difference between "dry" times and "dark" times. Dry times can result when we do not actively pursue our relationship with Jesus Christ because we are occupied with other matters. Surprisingly, "dark" times often occur when we are seeking the Lord and occupied with him. We know that we are in right relationship with him, yet our prayers seem to bounce back with complete silence.

Though there is great good that can come from these times, we need to guard against allowing our doubts and questions to diminish our desire to pray. When we feel this way, it is often because we have erected barriers that prevent us from experiencing God's power through prayer. Eventually they can discourage and defeat us.

So what are some of the questions that can turn into barriers if we don't endure them with patient expectation? I have encountered several. As we grapple with them, however, we can rest in God's great promise: "You will seek me and find me when you seek me with all your heart. I will be found by you" (Jeremiah 29:13-14).

How do I know that God really loves me?

Without a true understanding of God's love for you, your prayer life will never flourish. If you think God is mad at you, you will most likely withdraw and try to ignore him. If you think that you are not good enough for God, you will probably comment on how incapable you are and wallow in negative self-talk. If you do not truly believe that Jesus loves you, it will be difficult for you to attempt to do anything for him.

When you doubt God's love, you may become distant and aloof toward him. This creates a significant barrier. Doubts about God's love have been around since Satan first planted a lie in Eve's mind as they discussed a particular tree in the Garden of Eden.

I can imagine Satan saying to her, "Eve, if God really loved you, don't you think he would allow you to eat from *all* the trees?" She may have thought, *Hey, that's right. Maybe he doesn't love me like he said he did. If God loved us, why would he restrict us from this tree?*

We, like Adam and Eve, sometimes choose to believe that God does not have our best interests in mind. If you are like me, you may sometimes relate to your heavenly Father the way you related to your earthly father. I always felt like I had to earn my dad's love by performing well. How easy it is to project that onto God, even though he has none of the shortcomings of earthly fathers. In fact, he is far more loving than even the best earthly dad!

When I was a child, "Jesus Loves Me" was just a simple little song that I sang in Sunday school. A friend challenged me years ago to ask God to help me comprehend that he truly did love me just the way I was. Scripture helped me to understand that the phrase "Jesus loves me" is true and that Jesus sings this song over me and you!

Consider all the ways that God describes his love for you in Scripture:

- God will take great delight in you (Zephaniah 3:17).
- God will quiet you with his love (Zephaniah 3:17).
- God will rejoice over you with singing (Zephaniah 3:17).
- God loves you with an everlasting love (Jeremiah 31:3).
- We are called the apple of God's eye (Psalm 17:8).
- God says that "his banner over [us] is love" (Song of Songs 2:4). Wow, each of us is walking around with an invisible banner over our head that reads, "LOVED BY GOD" in capital letters.
- We are engraved on the palms of his hands (Isaiah 49:16).
- "How great is the love the Father has lavished on us" (1 John 3:1).
- A nursing mother may forget her child, but God will never forget us (Isaiah 49:15).
- He promises not to leave us as orphans (John 14:18).
- Nothing can separate us from the love of Christ (Romans 8:38-39).

Henry Blackaby noted: "God is far more interested in a love relationship with you than He is in what you can *do* for him. His desire is for you to love him."[15] If your love relationship with God is not right, nothing else, including your prayer time, will be all that it could be.

Even though I didn't always feel I was so important to God, I finally realized that he loves me as if I were the only person in the universe. He feels the same about you.

We must ask the Lord to help us bulldoze this barrier that keeps us from understanding how much God passionately loves each of us. No wonder the apostle Paul prays that we will "have power . . . to grasp how wide and long and high and deep is the love of Christ" (Ephesians 3:18). We need the Holy Spirit to give us the power to grasp this love, because it's unlike any other love we have experienced.

An interesting thing occurs as you begin to grasp from

Scripture how much the Lord Jesus loves you. He whispers his personal love to you through those Scriptures and he becomes more real to you. The more real he becomes to you, the more *you* love Jesus.

Why does it seem that God does not hear me when I pray?

Scripture repeatedly mentions that God *hears* our prayers (provided we are free from any known sin). He may not always answer them the way we hope, but we can count on him to hear them and, in his sovereignty, do what is best. This truth has been a faith booster for me.

When my husband and I have been asked to pray for someone who is terminally ill, our first desire is, of course, that the person will be healed. A few times my husband and I have seen God dramatically intervene in a person's life. Most of the time, however, God has healed these individuals by taking them home to be with him.

I remember kneeling by a bed when I was fourteen and earnestly telling the Lord to "please heal my mother from cancer." When I had finished, I got up and told my sister, "I know for sure that God is going to heal Mother." But God had plans for another kind of healing. She passed away a couple of days later. He had a perfect healing in mind for her—for her to be with him.

What I know now is that God did hear my request! He did not resent it when I told him in my childlike way what to do. He understood my human desire to keep my mother. How he must have cried with me during that petition, because he understood my loss as no one else could. "The Lord does not abandon anyone forever. Though he brings grief, he also shows compassion according to the greatness of his unfailing love. For he does not enjoy hurting people or causing them sorrow" (Lamentations 3:31-33, NLT). Although his answer was different from what I had asked, there is nothing wrong with his listening skills. I take great comfort in that!

"But God has surely listened and heard my voice in prayer" (Psalm 66:19). Oh, to trust that our sovereign God has indeed heard the cry of our hearts and can be trusted to do what is right! I keep this verse framed on the wall in my prayer closet: "Evening, morning and noon I cry out in distress, and *he hears my voice*" (Psalm 55:17, emphasis mine). How grateful I am for the assurance that God listens and hears us when we pray.

I don't give my children everything they ask me for. Sometimes I realize their desires are not in their best interest. How thankful I am that we have a heavenly Father who has never made a wrong decision and has never done anything to hurt us. My trust in Jesus' sovereignty and love smashes right through this barrier.

If God hears me, why does he seem so silent?

If you are currently asking this about your prayer life, I empathize. I know it is lonely, but keep going! You *will* come out of that dark, long tunnel with a deeper knowledge of God. This is a time when, in faith, you love him purely for who you know him to be—not just for what he can do for you or how he makes you feel.

Continue to *pursue* God! I have discovered that our Gardener uses such silences to prune his followers. If I relax and submit to his care, he will grow me deeper into him. Isn't that what I ultimately want—to go deeper into Christ?

To be candid, I am asking this question myself even as I write. A few months ago I remember crying out to the Lord all through the night concerning a church situation. I had been praying about it for months, and yet he had been quiet about the fervent, specific requests I brought to him. On this particular night I felt as if I were trying to hold on to God's royal robe. I told him that I was not going to let him go until he helped us. *Please, Father, rain down your Spirit on us. Please send someone to help us and someone to encourage my own heart. Please,*

please help us and show us what to do. Paul and I want your purposes to prevail, I begged.

I identified with Asaph, who wrote: "I cry out to God without holding back. Oh, that God would listen to me! When I was in deep trouble, I searched for the Lord. All night long I pray, with hands lifted toward heaven, pleading. There can be no joy for me until he acts. I think of God, and I moan, overwhelmed with longing for his help" (Psalm 77:1-3, NLT).

> *I will call upon God, and the Lord shall save me. Evening and morning and at noon I will pray, and cry aloud, and He shall hear my voice.*
> **Psalm 55:16-17,** NKJV

Although the Lord comforted me with such Scripture passages, I wanted to hear from God in a different way. In my humanness I desired his Holy Spirit to send me a personal message that everything was going to be okay. Oddly, along with the Scripture, a strange image kept coming to mind. Every so often, I pictured a pot of tulips.

That's strange, Father, I finally whispered to him in the quietness of the night. *Is there someone you would like me to send a pot of tulips to tomorrow?* There was only silence. I thought that perhaps the image represented my subconscious wish for our bitter cold February to turn to spring when the tulips would come up.

Eventually I fell asleep, still puzzling over the tulips while crying out to the Lord. When I awoke the next morning, I was tired from the fitful night of sleep. Again, however, the thought of tulips came to my mind.

"That is the strangest thing," I remarked out loud. I went down to our basement after our kids had left for school and began looking up the Scripture verses that had come to my attention during the night. One was Habakkuk 3:17-18, a passage my husband had recently preached on. The prophet Habakkuk wrote, *"Though* the fig tree does not bud . . . , *though* the olive crop fails . . . , *though* there are no sheep in the pen . . . , *yet* I will rejoice in the Lord" (emphasis mine).

Yet. What a beautiful word. *Lord,* I prayed, *there are so many thoughs right now in my life. Help me, even though I don't see you working, to have more* yets *to praise you no matter what.*

An hour and a half later I heard a knock. I opened the front door to see a deliveryman standing on my front porch. I quietly gasped when I saw him holding a pot of twelve pink tulips. I could barely thank him as he handed it to me. I quickly checked the card to see who had sent the tulips. They were from Lori Jo, a woman from our church. She had written a very encouraging note on the card.

I set the pot down on the kitchen table and cried. *Father, it is as if you sent Jesus to bring me these beautiful tulips on such a hard day.* I was swept away by the Father's love. I was reminded that even though God seemed silent about my requests, he *was* working. He also reminded me that he never withholds his love. He wanted me to know, too, that there are going to be days when there are no tulips, when God is silent and I will just need to accept his presence by faith.

After the delivery, I returned to the basement to look up the other passages that the Lord had brought to my mind the night before. As I looked up Isaiah 42:9 ("See, the former things have taken place, and new things I declare; before they spring into being I announce them to you"), the phone rang. Another woman from church was calling.

"Marilyn," Barb said, "I was cleaning my house when the Lord brought your name to my heart. I felt prompted to stop cleaning to call and encourage you."

"Oh, Barb," I exclaimed, "you cannot imagine how timely your phone call is!" I shared the strange but encouraging story of the tulips with her.

Barb responded, "Look outside right now and see what tulip bulbs have to endure." I looked out my kitchen window at the six inches or more of snow that lay on the ground. She continued, "You have tulip bulbs buried out there in all of this snow, but think about how they will spring up in May."

I gasped slightly and said, "When you called I was just meditating on the verse from Isaiah 42:9 about God doing a new thing, before it *springs* into being." The tulips fit that verse! The Lord knew I needed encouragement. I had gone to him first, and he sent me someone to order the tulips, a deliveryman to bring them to me, and a person to call just as I was trying to put everything together. What an awesome God we have!

My tulip bulbs triumphed over the harsh and snowy winter. Now there are beautiful pale pink tulips in my backyard.

A month ago, I talked with Lori Jo. We met at a local coffee shop, and I told her why her tulips were so meaningful to me. She offered some surprising details about ordering the flowers. She had felt impressed to send me flowers to encourage me. When she called the florist, she intended to order a mixed bouquet of spring flowers. The florist said they had a nice pot of pink tulips. Lori Jo did not want a pot of tulips, since tulips are so common in our city of Holland, Michigan.

She tried to tell the florist she'd rather order an arrangement with a variety of flowers. The florist kept pushing the pot of pink tulips, adding that they were ready for immediate delivery. Lori Jo said she still does not know how that determined florist talked her into sending the tulips! That was not *her* plan, but I know why those tulips were sent.

So the question remains: will I praise God in the silent times (even when he doesn't send a pot of tulips)? I pray I will. During these deepening and purifying times, we can abandon ourselves to the Lord Jesus and entrust ourselves to his care. We can ask the Lord to encourage us and thank him that he will speak to our heart and comfort us with his presence at some point. I now call these blackout periods the "ministry of dark times." I know that when the silence is lifted, I emerge with treasures that can only be mined in the dark, deep caverns of prayer.

Why doesn't God seem to answer some of my prayers?

I have a prayer request dating back to my first day of disciplined prayer on September 5, 1986. God has not answered that request yet. I believe it is a request that is right to pray about. However, I believe I have learned more about prayer from this one unanswered request than from all the answers I have received. That is because

- this request keeps me going back to God;
- it keeps me from getting a big head and thinking, *God answers* my *prayers when I pray for others;*
- it teaches me to wait *on* God while I am waiting *for* God to act;
- I do not sit around twiddling my thumbs, waiting for God to act. I wait *on* God by continually bringing my petition to him through prayer, searching the Word for guidance, and quietly listening for his voice.

God often teaches more through a prayer request he doesn't seem to answer right away than through one that he does. If you persevere, you will learn the secret of prevailing prayer, and you will learn to conform to God's timing and will. Finally, you will develop a deeper level of trust.

In his book *Too Busy Not to Pray,* Pastor Bill Hybels offers a concise summary of how God answers prayer:

If the request is wrong, God says, "No."
If the timing is wrong, God says, "Slow."
If you are wrong, God says, "Grow."
But if the *request,* the *timing,* and *you* are right,
God says, "Go."[16]

Prayer warrior George Müller once wrote out the steps he went through when seeking God's will on a matter. His principles continue to encourage me as I wait on the Lord to show me his guidance:

1. I seek at the beginning to get my heart into such a state that it has no will of its own in regard to a given matter.
2. I do not leave the result to feeling or simple impression.
3. I seek the Will of the Spirit of God through, or in connection with, the Word of God. The Spirit and the Word must be combined. If I look to the Spirit alone without the Word, I lay myself open to great delusions.
4. Next I take into account providential circumstances. These often plainly indicate God's Will in connection with His Word and Spirit.
5. I ask God in prayer to reveal His Will to me aright.
6. Thus, through prayer to God, the study of the Word, and reflection, I come to a deliberate judgment according to the best of my ability and knowledge, and if my mind is thus at peace, and continues so after two or three more petitions, I proceed accordingly.[17]

George Müller's journals reveal how he put these principles into practice. In the fall of 1845 he began praying to God for help in building an orphanage. That December he wrote how God used Scripture from Ezra to encourage him in his vision. A few days later he began to look at possible building sites. All were too expensive.

On January 31, 1846, he wrote: "It is now eighty-nine days since I have been daily waiting upon God about the building of an Orphan House. The Lord will soon give us a piece of ground." He continued to pray although he saw no answer.

Five days later, George talked to the landowner of one of the sites he had visited in early January. The man offered to sell him the land at a little more than half the price he had originally intended to charge. Müller was able to buy seven acres.[18]

What do Müller's guidelines have to do with unanswered prayer? To get my own heart in "such a state that it has no will of its own" is so important. I must wait for the request to be God's purpose and desire, and for the timing to be God's timing. Don't allow the barrier of unanswered prayer make you think that God doesn't care or that he has not taken notice of your petition. One of Müller's journal entries reads, "Finally, after I sought the help of God for *six hundred and seven days*, He has given me the desire of my heart" (emphasis mine).[19] This is what it means to pray through.

HELPS TO AID US AS WE PRAY

Understanding God's great love for us, even when he appears to be silent, is foundational to overcoming the barriers that can quench our desire to pray. While it's true that Satan seeks to discourage us, we do not fight against him alone. The Holy Spirit himself offers help for us as we pray. He desires to come alongside us in this adventure of listening prayer.

The Holy Spirit's prayers

First of all, the Holy Spirit *is* the "spirit of prayer." Amazingly, he prays through us and wants to do so. We have a built-in prayer guide! That means when we don't know how to pray about a matter, it's okay. The Holy Spirit knows our hearts and thoughts and can intercede for us in accordance with God's will. "In the same way, the Spirit helps us in our weakness. We do not know what we ought to pray for, but the Spirit himself intercedes for us with groans that words cannot express. And he who searches our hearts knows the mind of the Spirit, because the Spirit intercedes for the saints in accordance with God's will" (Romans 8:26-27).

I believe that by providing the gift of his Holy Spirit, God shows us once again how important prayer is to *him*. It is one thing to tell a person to go and do something that is difficult; it's another to come alongside someone to help.

The Word says that "God gives the Spirit without limit" (John 3:34). We can have the Holy Spirit in abundance to help us pray.

Prayer burden

When I sense a continual heaviness to pray for someone or something, it is most likely because the Holy Spirit has given me a *prayer burden*. He is asking me to join him in prayer, and he does the equipping. This again is a time for listening prayer. I must pray about this concern until I feel released, or until I do not feel the "weight" of that prayer need on me.

When you feel a burden to pray but are not sure why, ask: *God, what do you want me to pray for? What is it that you desire to accomplish that needs my prayer?*

When you know that God wants you to pray about something but aren't sure how to pray, ask that the Father may be glorified. God will always take the route that brings him the greatest glory. That "the Father may be glorified" (John 14:13, NKJV) is the supreme motive of all praying.

For many weeks last year, the Lord kept putting it on my heart to intercede on behalf of our church. I did not know why, but I sensed an urgency to pray. The weight of this was very heavy, and many times I was pleading with tears pouring down my cheeks. I asked the Holy Spirit to help me in my praying, while at the same time thanking Jesus that he too was interceding for us.

Looking back, I know why I was under that weight to pray. We were about to face significant changes and challenges in our fellowship, and Satan was going to throw some fiery darts. I believe that the Spirit of God alerted me to pray even though I did not know yet what was going on.

More often, there will be times you feel "heavy" with a prayer burden, and you know exactly why you are to pray. This happened to me not too many months ago. Our church needed a worship leader. We desired an individual who was a person of prayer and relied on the Word of God daily. True, we wanted someone who was gifted, but we especially needed one whose heart was fully devoted to God. How could a worship leader stand in front of our congregation to lead us if he or she was not spending significant time with God first?

I was in earnest intercession about this burden for days. It didn't seem to matter what I was doing—at various times I was prompted to pray about that need. It also affected me during the night. Often I would awaken and silently cry out to the Lord: *Lord Jesus, have mercy on us. We don't know who this individual is, but you do. Would you please help us and send us the person of your choosing?* I pleaded with the Lord over and over again during the night hours. A couple of weeks later the weight of that request lifted.

This prayer had not yet been answered when I sensed the Lord releasing me from the *intensity* of that kind of praying. I continued to pray about it, but the weight of that request was gone. I felt a deep assurance that God had answered that prayer and I was to focus on praising and thanking him for his answer.

I desire to be faithful in prayer when the Spirit of God places one of his burdens on me, and to pray for as long as he desires. These prayer burdens are a tremendous privilege, an opportunity to listen to the Holy Spirit, and a time to partner with God.

I cannot begin to understand the burden of prayer that our Lord Jesus himself bears from moment to moment. I do know, however, that by allowing the Lord to place his concerns on your heart, you will see a little bit of his heart for prayer.

Crying out to the Lord

Crying out to the Lord happens many times in conjunction with a prayer burden. It is not something you do to try to get God to hear you better. I believe that when we are desperate for God and feel that pull to prayer, our heart naturally cries out, "Abba, Father." It is during these times that "the Holy Spirit prays for us with such feeling that it cannot be expressed in words" (Romans 8:26, TLB).

Over and over I have found that when I cry out to the Lord, I end up lying facedown on the carpet of my prayer closet. This happens when I am completely depending on the Lord Jesus. It is a body position that is meant to communicate that I am bowing to the Lord of lords, not only with my body, but also with my heart. It's not that I think God is more likely to answer my prayer because I'm stretched out before him; rather, I want him to know that my heart desires to talk with his and that I want what *he* wants. I lay down whatever rights I believe are mine and seek to humble myself. It is a form of reverent submission. I am desperate for God's way! It is often during these intense times of crying out to the Lord that he speaks peace and hope to my heart.

Yesterday, while I was reading through the list of the Hebrew tribes in 1 Chronicles 5, I discovered a significant verse almost lost in that list of names. The passage mentions that the tribes from Reuben, Gad, and Manasseh were helped in a war "because they *cried out* to [God] during the battle. He answered their prayers, because they trusted in him" (v. 20, emphasis mine).

The book of Hebrews talks about how even Jesus, during his days on earth, "offered up prayers and petitions with loud cries and tears to the one who could save him from death, and he was heard because of his reverent submission" (5:7). It is right to cry out to the Lord! "Trust in him at all times, O people; *pour out* your hearts to him, for God is our refuge" (Psalm 62:8, emphasis mine).

Prayer of relinquishment

There are times to "give up" in prayer. Sounds contradictory, doesn't it? These are the times the Lord asks us during our prayer time: *Are you willing to give up that something or someone you are praying about?* If we are not listening to the Lord, we can miss this quiet but penetrating question.

Currently our three eldest daughters and their husbands are all in seminary studying for the ministry. Recently my husband and I were out having lunch with some friends. They asked us how we were praying for our married kids since they would all be completing their seminary training soon. "Are you praying that they all move closer to you?" they asked.

I replied, "You know, I have had to pray relinquishment prayers on their behalf. I would love for them to live near to us! They are our dearest friends. However, as I have prayed for them, I sense that I need to release them so they are free to go wherever the Lord leads them. They must do God's kingdom work where he places them. I cannot hold so tightly to them." I have to remind myself that my children belong to the Lord; they are only on loan to my husband and me. They are *God's,* and he loves them even more than we do.

Relinquishment prayers are difficult ones to pray. Yet, I have found that when I relinquish my desires to the Lord, he often has a better plan. In other cases the Lord gets me to the point at which I finally relinquish my desires, and then he unexpectedly gives what I desired back to me. This happened with our son years ago.

Paul was sixteen months old, and our family of seven was traveling to New York with a side trip to Canada. Just as we were getting ready to cross the border from Michigan into Canada, our son went into convulsions and stopped breathing.

My husband quickly pulled the car over and told the border patrol that we needed emergency medical help. The guard called an ambulance. Paul was lifeless in my arms as we waited.

> *Father . . . may your will be done.*
> *Matthew 6:9-10, NLT*

As soon as the medical team arrived, they hooked Paul up to oxygen and started working on him. They told me to get in the front seat of the ambulance while the rest of the family was to follow them in our van. I will never forget sitting in that ambulance with my eyes glued to our small son. He was hooked up to all kinds of tubes. A female nurse softly repeated, "Come on, honey, breathe. Please breathe, little honey." Time seemed to stop as I watched our son's small body.

Lord Jesus, I cried out in my heart, *you gave us Paul Matthew. I don't want him to die; we have had him such a short time. I know, however, that he is yours. I release him to you; there is nothing I can do.* Nothing within me wanted to let him go. Yet I was totally helpless, and releasing him to Jesus was the only thing I could do for our baby.

In our case, the Lord restored Paul to us after many anxious days. However, I know many families who have had to relinquish their loved ones and are waiting to join them in heaven. I learned through this experience that to relinquish and leave the results to God, no matter what happens, brings the most peace. I can do so, not because I am fatalistic, but because I am confident in the trustworthiness of a loving, sovereign God.

I admit that I have had to pray relinquishment prayers concerning material things as well. For the first thirteen years of marriage, Paul and I did not own our home. We lived in college and seminary housing for the first four years and parsonages for the next nine. Before moving into the first parsonage, we asked the church board if we could possibly have our own home. A few board members met with us. One said to us, "Well, frankly, there are several of us who feel like you are not ready to own your own home." That was a blow to our pride!

I keenly remember the disadvantages of living in that first parsonage. It was on a very busy street that was also a truck route. We almost lost one of our daughters on that street. Unknown to me, our two-year-old had quietly slipped out the door while I was on the phone and headed to the street. Some yelling caught my attention, and I looked out our glass side door. Our neighbor was running past our house yelling, "There's a baby in the street! There's a baby in the street!" I looked to see whose baby he was chasing. To my horror, I saw him racing after our daughter Mandy, who was running straight for the traffic. I ran out the door and began to scream for her, praying that she would hear me above the noise of the cars. Fortunately, our neighbor scooped her up when she was about two feet into the road. Amazingly, there was a space between all the cars and trucks! That event intensified my desire to move. I wanted out of there so badly!

I was tired of the constant noise from traffic. Every truck that passed our house made our windows rattle. A houseguest commented one morning that during the night he had thought a jet plane was coming into his room. "Those trucks are loud! How do you guys ever get any sleep?"

There were two large bedrooms. Our three children occupied one room, while Paul and I had the other. When guests came, we housed them as well.

It seems silly now, but I complained about living there. It didn't help that one of our parishioners came over one day and said, "It doesn't seem right that *you* live here. Our old pastor and family should still be here." Ouch! I am ashamed to say that I complained to the Lord the entire seven years we lived there!

Finally, the church board said that they were going to sell the current parsonage and look for a larger parsonage for us once the old one sold. *Hopefully,* I thought, *we will have more bedrooms in the next house.* The parsonage was put on the market, but after eight months without a sale, I knew I had to give up my desire, not only of living in our own home, but also of living in a different parsonage. The real estate agent told us that our parsonage was a very difficult house to sell because of the high level of traffic and noise. Since the church could not buy another parsonage until the old one sold, we waited.

I still prayed about it, but I quit complaining and relinquished all my desires about housing to the Lord. The next month the parsonage sold, and the board purchased a nice home for us just in time for the birth of our fourth child. Years later God provided a wonderful home of our own—beyond what I would have ever asked for. Looking back, I see how the Lord was preparing an earthly home for us. Knowing what I know now, I wish I had relinquished my desires to him sooner!

Sometimes God may ask you to relinquish your right to "be right" in a relational conflict. That's really hard! I know a couple who believe their daughter is marrying the wrong man. He is not walking with the Lord, and they fear for their daughter. The daughter, however, will not listen. She believes that she will be able to change him after they get married.

The parents have some options. They can withdraw from her, argue and fight with her, or release her into the Lord's hands. These parents have sought to relinquish their desires about this to the Lord. Do they still pray that she will change her mind? Yes. However, they have said all that they can say to her. They are still concerned, but they are not allowing their worry or disappointment to consume them. They are asking the Lord to help them adjust to and love their soon-to-be son-in-law.

Relinquishing people or situations to the Lord gives him freedom to work as he desires in our lives. D. L. Moody said, "Spread out your petition before God and then say, 'Thy will, not mine, be done.' The sweetest lesson I have learned in God's school is to let the Lord choose for me."[20] Instead of interfering, fretting, and getting frustrated, we cooperate with him. We must continually listen to him as we turn over our deepest hopes and desires to the Lord.

The question that the Lord sets before me whenever I am tenaciously holding on to something or someone is, *Marilyn, do you love me above every person, place, or thing?* I then go through the list of all those I love. I name my husband and our children. Do I love them above God? What place (that could mean a location or a position) am I seeking right now? Is that consuming my thoughts above God? What thing (material, physical, or emotional) do I want right now? Is the desire for that greater than my desire for the Lord? Many times I will ask myself, *What am I thinking about the most these days?* These reflections show me what has captured my heart. I then say, *Lord Jesus, I relinquish all of these desires so that you will be first in my heart and life.*

Prayers of relinquishment help me to deny my own desires and die to self. Jesus prayed a prayer of relinquishment in the garden of Gethsemane. He shared his desires with his heavenly Father and then listened. Jesus did not receive the answer he prayed for. He first said, "Please take this cup of suffering away from me," but then added, "Yet I want your will, not mine" (Mark 14:36, NLT). Look what his prayer of relinquishment brought us! Jesus knows what it is like to relinquish our desires.

Touching God through our prayers

Not long ago, it occurred to me that our prayers, aided by the Holy Spirit, can also touch the heart of God. That is an amazing thought. To think we can actually connect to the God of the universe through prayer. What a powerful link!

Recently my husband was preaching on the passage about the woman who had been hemorrhaging for twelve years (Luke

8:42-48). She was desperate to be healed by Jesus. The day she sought him out, the crowds were packed in around him. The Bible says that "the crowds almost crushed [Jesus]."

She had probably hoped all day that she would be touched and healed by Jesus. It did not look possible, though. There were too many people. She devised another plan. Could she push her way through all of those people so *she* could touch Jesus?

What made this woman go through so much trouble to get to Jesus? Her desperation! She could have been weakened by all of her bleeding and decided she was just too tired to continue making her way through the crowds. Yet she pressed and pushed until she was finally close enough to touch the edge of his cloak. Did she collapse at his feet? She was obviously low enough to the ground to be able to touch the hem of his garment.

As soon as she touched him, she was instantly healed. She knew it and so did Jesus! He asked, "Who touched me?"

Peter answered, "Master, the people are crowding and pressing against you."

But Jesus replied, "Someone touched me; I know that power has gone out from me."

After the woman admitted what she had done, Jesus responded, "Daughter, your faith has healed you. Go in peace."

My point is this: so often we say to the Lord, *Lord Jesus, bless me. Bless my efforts and come and touch me.* Are we desperate enough that we say to the Lord, *Let me just get close to you so I can touch* you? I think the Lord must be pleased—even blessed—when we initiate touching him. It shows our desperation and shows that we want him. I truly believe that prayer is a way to touch Jesus. It may not always be easy. Your phone may interrupt you at the office, the doorbell may ring, there will be unexpected interruptions, and there will always be someone or something pressing and crowding in on you to keep you from touching Jesus. But when you do touch Jesus through prayer, his power goes out to you.

I don't want to do things in my own power. I want to touch Jesus, and I want to walk in the power of the Holy Spirit. Be listening for the Lord as you reach out to touch him. Never be satisfied until you get into personal contact with Jesus Christ.

Fasting

Fasting, or abstaining from something to concentrate on our walk with the Lord, can also serve as a prompt to pray. I call fast days my "feast on Jesus" days. I am much more aware of him on those days. One way of fasting from food is to fast from after an evening meal to the following evening meal. (Be sure to check with your doctor before you fast.)

Fasting doesn't have to be only from food. I recently heard someone say that she was going to spend the next forty days fasting from gossip. When asked how she was going to do that, she replied that there were three steps. First, whenever she heard anything negative said about someone she would not contribute to that conversation. Second, she would say something positive concerning the person being talked about, and third, she would pray for that person.

Another way to fast is to quit talking. A few months ago while I was speaking at a retreat in Nebraska, I had five free hours that I had not planned on. With the Lord's prompting, I decided to fast from talking during those hours. I had not done that before. It was a rich time alone with the Lord. No phone calls, no TV. . . just silence. God spoke to my heart, and I felt refreshed and filled with the Holy Spirit. Normally, when I am through teaching at a weekend retreat, I am exhausted both physically and emotionally. Usually, I have an adrenaline letdown and become very self-critical. I left this particular retreat, however, feeling full of energy. I was not even tired. The time I had spent listening to God and refraining from talking had been very restoring for me.

At the airport on my way home, I began talking with a couple in line with me. "What brings you out to Nebraska?" the husband asked.

"I just finished speaking at a retreat in Grand Island," I answered.

"Oh," said the wife, "what did you speak about?"

"I spoke about forgiveness," I casually replied. The husband and wife looked at each other. I couldn't read their expressions, but they were communicating something with their eyes. After we checked through security I sat down to wait for our flight.

Soon the wife of the couple I had just been talking to asked if she could sit next to me while we waited for our plane. She said, "You're a Christian, aren't you?"

"Yes," I replied.

"I am too, and I was wondering if I could talk to you about something." I nodded.

"I'm struggling with forgiveness right now." She broke down in tears, and I waited until she could continue. "I am really hurting, and my husband and I couldn't believe that you said you had just spoken on forgiveness. He encouraged me to come over and talk with you." She continued to weep as she relayed her story. She was frustrated with God because she felt that he had let her down. She also struggled to know what to do about her career because it took her away from her husband for weeks at a time. After I listened, it was like the Lord Jesus gave me the words to share with her.

As I prayed silently for help, I sensed I was to ask her this question: "Do you know for certain that you are in the Lord's will right now?"

She was quiet for a moment and then said, "No, I *know* I'm not in God's will. That is the problem. I know what he wants me to do, but I am not ready to do it yet." She stood up after a while to go to the restroom and wipe her tear-stained face.

While she was gone, a young couple who were also waiting for the plane came over to me and said, "We are sorry to interrupt, but we couldn't help overhearing you and that other woman. We are also Christians and we just want you to know that we are praying for you as you share with her." I thanked them, and we commented on how wonderful it was to find fellow believers all over the world.

The woman returned to finish our conversation. The words the Lord gave me to share with that woman had come out of my time of silence with him! The Lord had spoken to me on the issue of forgiveness during my silent time, and it fit her situation as well. I was able to pass on some of the Scriptures I had read during my time alone. I'm also certain our time together was influenced by the young couple who sat praying for us.

The woman e-mailed me when she got home to say that she and her husband had done some talking and she was so thankful for the Scriptures I had shared with her. She now desired to do what the Lord wanted her to do.

Perhaps there is something that the Spirit of God has impressed on you to fast from. Using part of your day to fast, pray, and listen is a wonderful way to keep your thoughts on him.

The Holy Spirit has taught me so much about prayer as I have cried out to him, said prayers of relinquishment, sought to touch the heart of God, and fasted. Yet I have so much more to learn! In fact, the more I learn, the more I realize that I will never totally understand this wonderful privilege called prayer. It was through prayer that the Lord first touched my life and opened up a fuller, deeper way to know him. In those early days of desiring to have a life of prayer, the Lord sent a simple caterpillar into our family to teach us even more.

CHAPTER 9

Capturing the Spirit of Prayer: Slinky the Caterpillar

While I've learned much about prayer from the great prayer warriors of the past and present, some of the most profound lessons came from a fuzzy caterpillar named Slinky.

One month after I first set aside a daily time for prayer, the Lord sent this caterpillar into our daughter Christy's life. Christy was ten at the time. Her best friend, Heather, gave her the caterpillar after walking with her parents to our home one beautiful fall Sunday afternoon.

"Mom, look what Heather just gave me. May I please keep him?" Christy asked.

"Oh, Christy," I replied, "this is late fall and the caterpillar needs to stay outside to do whatever caterpillars do in the winter."

"Please," begged Christy. "If I can find a jar in the basement, may I keep Slinky in the house?"

Oh, dear, now the caterpillar has a name, I thought. As I

looked into her hopeful dark brown eyes, I finally relented, but I made sure she knew that I thought it should be set free. I felt sorry for the poor thing.

Christy quickly located a jar in the basement and placed a climbing twig inside. She filled the bottom of his new home with caterpillar food—grass and leaves—and lovingly placed Slinky in the glass jar. "Look, Mom," Christy excitedly exclaimed, "Slinky is crawling up the twig. He likes it!" Sure enough, Slinky put on a show, and Christy invited her neighbor friends over to see her new pet.

Not long after that, Slinky began to form a cocoon on the twig he had climbed. The neighborhood children returned several times to watch Slinky's transformation. It was as if he had traded his stylish fuzzy coat for a hard old leather jacket.

The months went on. The grass and leaves in the bottom of the jar withered and dried up. Slinky now looked like a small brown Tootsie Roll stuck on a twig. The visits from the neighbor kids became infrequent.

One day in December while decorating our home for the holidays, I asked Christy if I could please move Slinky off our dining-room buffet. She reluctantly mumbled her okay, and I quickly put Slinky in a kitchen cupboard before she could change her mind. *Maybe she will forget about him,* I thought. There was no way Slinky could still be alive—not after all of this time. I thought perhaps it was best to just leave Slinky in the cupboard after the holidays. Christy would eventually realize that he had died, and time would help soften the blow.

Christmas and New Year's Day came and went. No one mentioned Slinky. Early in January, I reached inside a cupboard for a water pitcher. As I did, something caught my eye. Something was moving in the back of the cupboard. It was Slinky, trying to get out of his cocoon! "Everybody come to the kitchen," I yelled, "Slinky is hatching! Slinky is hatching!"

I set the jar on our kitchen island so we could all have a

better view. The children ran in just in time to watch Slinky, the ordinary caterpillar, emerge as a gorgeous butterfly. This was not the ugly moth that someone had suggested it might be. It was beautiful! The vibrant blues and oranges outlined in black on his wings contrasted sharply with the drab lifeless color of the empty chrysalis lying on the bottom of the jar.

> *The earnest prayer of a righteous person has great power and wonderful results.*
> **James 5:16, NLT**

We were elated! We had had our own personal viewing of the metamorphosis. Slinky flapped his wings, not only to dry them but to show off as well. After dinner, Christy called all the neighborhood children. A stream of kids paraded in to witness the new life of Slinky the *butterfly.*

In the middle of this elation it dawned on me that Slinky was not going to live. I looked out our living-room window. Mounds of fresh snow were evidence of a recent Michigan blizzard. The butterfly needed to fly—it needed freedom from the glass jar that held it captive. But Slinky also required a warm habitat—something we could not supply.

Later that evening I went upstairs to say good night to Christy. Her cheeks were still flushed from the excitement of watching a caterpillar transform into a butterfly. "Mom," she said happily, "I want to take Slinky to school tomorrow to show him to my class."

I knew I had to break the sad news to her. "That's a good idea," I replied. "But, Christy, I need to tell you something. Slinky is not going to make it, honey." I said it as tenderly as I could.

Her face took on a very puzzled look. "But why not, Mom?"

"Honey, look out your bedroom window. Slinky can't survive outside. I thought about letting him fly around in the basement, but he wouldn't be happy doing that. He needs to be outside in warm weather."

In all her excitement, Christy had not even thought about the weather. "Oh!" she groaned.

Christy then said something that I will never forget. "Mom, you know how you have been talking about how important it is to pray?"

Hesitantly I answered yes.

"Well, I know that you have been getting up early to pray in the laundry room, because I've come downstairs a couple of times and I've seen you praying." That was news to me. I had no idea that Christy had caught me in prayer. "Could we please pray that God will spare Slinky's life?" Christy's eyes shone with hope and childlike faith.

How I hated to disappoint her. I swallowed hard. "Christy, yes, of course we can pray for Slinky, but sometimes God doesn't answer our requests the way we want him to. Sometimes he has other plans." I was trying to give God all kinds of "outs" so Christy would not be disappointed when God did not answer her request. I had to make God look good.

My thoughts whirled silently. *God, please don't let her down. Not now. Not when I have impressed on our children the importance of prayer. They are going to think that I am wrong about your wanting us to pray. I don't see any possible way for you to answer her prayer, but would you in some way reward her childlike trust in you?*

I asked Christy to pray first. Actually I needed a couple of seconds to pull my heart together. I also wanted to see how she was going to pray. "Dear Jesus," Christy began, "please spare Slinky's life." Her prayer was simple and earnest.

When it was my time to pray I asked that *if* it was God's will (that was a safe request) that he would work out a way to spare Slinky's life. I wanted so much to protect God's reputation! I must admit that I doubted God would come through on something so insignificant. When I finished praying, we wiped away our tears and hugged each other good night.

The next morning, Slinky was still merrily flapping his wings in his glass prison. *Well, at least he is still alive,* I told the Lord. Christy carefully wrapped Slinky's jar in a towel to keep him warm until she could get to the school bus stop down the street. We said good-bye and Christy closed the front door behind her. Moments later I heard the front door open again.

"Mom?" she called, sticking her head back through the door. "Pleeeeeeease pray for Slinky today."

"I am, honey," I reassured her, but my own heart was silently sinking.

I was busy trying to clean up the house and care for the baby when the phone rang. I answered rather absentmindedly.

"Hi, Marilyn, this is Judy. How are you today?"

"Oh, not so good," I told my neighbor.

"What's wrong?" she asked.

"You know that caterpillar we had on our buffet?" She had seen him many times as a cocoon.

"Yes," she replied.

"Well, Slinky hatched last night and he is a gorgeous butterfly."

"Hey, that's great news! Why do you sound down?"

"Judy, look outside! Where is this butterfly supposed to go?"

"Oh," she responded. There was a moment of silence and then Judy exclaimed, "I know what we can do! The main reason I called was to tell you that I was going away for a few days, and I just wanted to say good-bye. Marilyn, I am flying by private jet to Fort Myers, Florida, later this afternoon. I could take Slinky to Florida with me!"

I could not believe it. "Are you serious, Judy?"

"Yes, of course. I would love to do that."

I had had no idea she was going away. To me there had been no answers for Slinky. Now, God had just provided a way to save Slinky.

That afternoon Christy and Slinky came home from school. I was amazed that Slinky was still alive. He was still flapping his wings and had made quite a debut in the classroom. "Christy, I've got great news for you—Slinky is going to live!"

Her face was incredulous. "What happened, Mom?"

"Judy is flying out to Florida in a few minutes and will take Slinky with her so he can live there."

For just a moment she seemed sad as she realized she was going to have to let Slinky go. However, she quickly became very excited. "God answered our prayers," she sang out jubilantly.

Actually, I said silently to the Lord, *I believe you answered Christy's prayer, which was offered in childlike trust. Thank you, however, for answering my "lack of faith" prayer. You are an incredible God!*

Christy spent the next couple of minutes saying good-bye to Slinky. She then wrapped up the glass jar and hugged it before walking across the street to Judy's house. Judy promised to take some pictures of Slinky's release.

The next week Judy returned home and as promised gave us pictures of Slinky. She had had someone take a picture as she unscrewed the lid. Slinky, as if on cue, fluttered out of the jar and perched himself on Judy's hand. Slinky sat on her hand for a few moments, sunning himself in the warm Florida sunshine. Another picture shows Slinky soaring off into the blue skies. Slinky was free, and we had learned some valuable lessons about prayer.

The Lord spoke to our entire family through our experiences with Slinky. Does God care about butterflies? Yes! Does God care about a child's request? Yes! Does God care about you? Yes, yes, yes.

Not long after that incident, Christy came to me. Slinky had profoundly affected her. "Mom, I see now how important it is to pray about everything. I want to start praying every day."

A year later, Holly, who is two years younger than Christy, said to me, "I have watched Christy pray since last January and now I want to too." These two girls influenced their younger siblings as well.

It continues to amaze me that the Lord used a little butterfly to teach our children the importance of prayer. They caught the *discipline* and the *spirit* of prayer.

What will it take for your prayer life to soar to greater heights? Yes, God cares about butterflies, but he cares about you more than you can imagine. Prayer is your opportunity to talk to God. Listening is his opportunity to speak back to your heart. Pray—and then listen.

What is prompting you to pray? An illness? A troubled relationship? A gnawing sense that something is missing in your life? Perhaps your prompt is as small as a butterfly. Regardless of what it is, the only way to enter into a vibrant prayer life is by beginning to pray. Just do it! Your life will never be the same.

In part 1 we saw that the Lord gives us *purpose* when we are in his *Word*. In part 2 we saw that the Lord gives us *power* through *prayer*. In part 3 we will see how the Lord *partners* with us when we *listen* to his voice.

QUESTIONS TO THINK ABOUT:

1. If Jesus asked you today if you could watch with him for one hour, what would you say?
2. Do you have a set appointment with God each day? If so, keep it up! If not, what steps could you take to begin one?
3. Think back to the five *Ds*: *desire, decision, discipline, delight,* and *daily*. In which of these areas is the Lord prompting you to develop your prayer life?
4. Are you giving God your *leftover* time or your *best* time? How do your actions show that?
5. As you pray, do you spend time both talking and listening? If not, how can you begin to incorporate both?
6. Have you ever tried praying specific Scripture verses? Describe your experience.
7. What are some of the ways you pray *throughout* your day?
8. Do you think any of the "traps" mentioned in chapter 6 are keeping you from developing a regular prayer life? If so, which one(s)? How can you learn to avoid these traps?
9. Have you ever sought God with all your heart during a dark period but felt as if your prayers just bounced back? Did this experience strengthen or discourage you? What did you learn about God through it?
10. Have you ever felt a prayer burden or prayed a prayer of relinquishment for someone or something? If so, describe it. How did it affect your prayer life?

Recognizing God's Voice
While Listening

PART 3

CHAPTER 10

Stopping to Listen

*I*n the spring of 1993, I was asked to write and record some short radio spots for a small Christian organization. I was to give a series of one-minute stories from my life to demonstrate how God works in an ordinary homemaker's day. I had not asked for the assignment, nor did I really want it.

What do I have to say? I asked myself. After praying about it, however, I could see no valid reason to say no other than my own fear of failure. Reluctantly, I agreed to write several stories.

Soon after, I was told the radio spots were being discontinued because the manager had resigned. While I was relieved at not having to do any more radio tapings, I also felt frustrated. I had definitely stepped out of my comfort zone, and I had faced my biggest fear—failure.

Why, Lord, I questioned, *would you put me through all of that when you knew how difficult it was for me?*

I heard a faint familiar whispering in the back of my mind:

Go back and read the stories you wrote in your notebook. That was it—plain, simple, and yet compelling. Curiously, I paged through my notebook and began to read story after story. And then I saw it—all of my stories had to do with listening to God!

I had never before thought about sitting quietly and listening to God, but that was precisely what the Holy Spirit was about to teach me. He was preparing me for one of the biggest adventures in my life: spiritual dialogue. God got my attention by taking some of the most insignificant, mundane, and at times even absurd moments of my life and turning them into life-changing encounters. The following two illustrations come from my notebook of stories.

PUMPKIN BREAD FOR MRS. DAWSON

One evening when I was expecting company to come for dinner, I decided to bake my straight-from-the-pumpkin bread, which was a family favorite. I pulled the frozen pumpkin pulp out of the freezer and began mixing the ingredients. Just as I was adding the baking soda, I was interrupted with an out-of-the-blue thought that I could not explain. *Share one of those pumpkin bread loaves with Mrs. Dawson.*

Where did that come from? I wondered. The crazy thought came again.

But, I reasoned silently, *I need both of those loaves of bread for our company. One won't be enough!* The prompting continued. I could not remember a time when I had felt such a strong compulsion to stop what I was doing and make an adjustment.

Lord, is this you trying to get my attention? I finally asked. *You know that I am having a large group over tonight, and I need both loaves of bread.* The gentle impression from the Lord continued. I gave in.

As soon as the bread was cool enough to pack, I wrapped up a loaf and drove it over to Mrs. Dawson, a senior who lived a few blocks away. As I walked up the path to her front door, I could see her through the picture window. She was napping. Quietly opening her front door, I set the bread down in her entryway with a note and left. Returning home, I finished preparing the rest of the dinner, hoping I would have enough bread to serve our guests.

Shortly before our company arrived, the phone rang. It was Mrs. Dawson. "Marilyn," she began, "thank you so much for the pumpkin bread. I have very little food in the house, and I didn't know what I was going to eat for dinner tonight. Your bread is like a gift from heaven."

I gasped quietly. Little did she know it *was* a gift from heaven! "Lord," I said out loud after I hung up the phone, "I almost missed it. I almost missed obeying the prompting of your Holy Spirit. I didn't know Mrs. Dawson needed food, but you did! Please help me to pay more attention to you throughout my day. Don't let me miss what you want me to do." (By the way, the Lord took care of me too. We had more than enough pumpkin bread—one loaf was the perfect amount for our dinner that evening.)

WHISPERS FROM GOD IN AISLE TWO

One morning a few weeks later, I headed to the grocery store to pick up a few items for a pastors' wives luncheon. Along the way I sensed the Holy Spirit prompting me to turn in to the bank to cash a check I had received as a gift from a friend.

Am I imagining this? I wondered. As silly as it may sound, I did not want to cash my check. I knew that as soon as I did, it would probably go toward school field trips, lunch money, or some fund-raiser. I liked the idea of carrying around the thirty-dollar check because it made me feel like I had some spending money.

I argued with myself, but the prompting only intensified. *If I to go to the bank,* I thought, *it makes more sense for me to go after I go to the grocery store.* But I just couldn't shake the feeling that I needed to go to the bank first. *Perhaps this is the Lord prompting me as he did with Mrs. Dawson,* I reasoned. So I reluctantly pulled in to the bank entrance. After I cashed the check, I drove to the grocery store, still thinking I had just done a strange thing.

In aisle two I ran into Jane from church. "Hi, Jane," I said cheerily.

"Hello," came her rather glum reply.

"What's wrong?" I asked. Jane told me that she needed food for her four children and did not have enough money to buy groceries. All of a sudden it was as if Jane's voice faded and I heard the Lord's voice loud and clear. *Give her the thirty dollars—that is why I had you cash your check.*

Immediately I began fumbling in my purse for the money. Handing her the thirty dollars, I blurted, "Here, Jane, this is for you. Do not pay me back. Believe me; I know you are supposed to have it."

Jane was bewildered at first. Then as tears trickled down her cheeks, she told me that prior to going to the store she had searched under couch cushions and various other places looking for loose change so she could buy groceries. After finding a small amount of change, she had driven to the store. Before going in, she had sat in her car in the parking lot, held up the change to the Lord, and asked him to help her get the groceries they needed.

By now we were hugging and I was crying with her. I'm sure that the people who were trying to get around us were wondering what was going on. I too wondered what had just happened.

Later that day, I began to question the whole incident. *Lord, did I do the right thing in giving her the money?* I was not used to listening to the prompting of the Lord; it was so new to me. *Perhaps,* I thought, *I just "enabled" my friend.* Yet as soon as that idea popped into my mind, I brushed it away. No, I knew Jane, and she was not that kind of person. She would never ask anyone for money.

Feeling confused, I asked the Lord to please let me know that what had happened was of him. I needed confirmation! As I prayed about this, the Lord brought a verse to my thoughts. "Suppose a brother or sister is without clothes and daily food. If one of you says to him, 'Go, I wish you well; keep warm and well fed,' but does nothing about his physical needs, what good is it?" (James 2:15-16). The verse helped me a bit. Besides, I rationalized, even if it had not been the Spirit's prompting, at least I had helped someone.

> *[God] forms the mountains, creates the wind, and reveals his thoughts to man.*
> **Amos 4:13**

The Lord, however, was not finished. A couple of days later I received a card in the mail with a check for forty dollars. It was from my friend Kathleen, who lived in California. "Marilyn," she wrote, "it occurred to me that I don't know when your birthday is and I wanted to send you a check for your day whenever it is." (This was the fall, and my birthday wasn't until January.) I realized that the Lord had given my thirty-dollar-check back with a ten dollar bonus!

I'm not suggesting that the Lord always pays you back in monetary ways, but he always blesses obedience. He knew that this whole idea of "paying attention" was new to me and he wanted me to be more alert to his leading.

SETTING THE STAGE FOR LISTENING

As I reread other stories in my notebook, I noticed that each one had a common thread running through it—listening. *Lord, I prayed, I believe you prompted me to read this notebook so I could see that you want me to be open to listening to you on a daily basis—not just for specialized, isolated events, but all day long.* I closed the notebook I was reading and realized that the

Lord was opening a whole new way of living out ordinary days with his extraordinary power.

I had never heard a sermon on listening to God, nor had I read any books on the subject. While at certain times I had definitely sensed the Lord's leading in my life, I had concluded that he provided it only at special times.

I remember going into the bathroom where my mother was brushing her hair when I was nine. "Mother," I said, "I really think that God told me he wants me to marry a minister when I grow up."

She smiled and said, "Well then, we better send you off to a college where they make ministers." Putting down her hairbrush, she turned to me and said, "Marilyn, I know that for you too." I skipped out of the room with a sense of peace—my mom already knew what I had just told her. For me, this was a very real and definite calling from the Lord.

Another significant moment when I sensed his leading occurred early in my marriage. My husband was in seminary, preparing for pastoral ministry. I became sick and assumed I was pregnant. The lab tests showed, however, that I was not expecting. We were puzzled, and I became increasingly ill. Finally my doctor sent me to a medical center for major testing. Many X rays were taken, but still, nothing showed up. I continued to be extremely ill. Something was wrong.

On an impulse, the doctor ordered another pregnancy test after the first test and sent it to a different lab. The test results came back positive. There had been an error in the first lab report. I was approximately six weeks along. Our jubilation quickly turned to fear when three different doctors warned us of a grim outcome if I continued the pregnancy. Their advice was unanimous: "Abort this fetus; you have had extensive radiation." We consulted three other specialists, and they said to go ahead and keep the baby. We did not know what to do.

The year was 1975, and not many Christians were talking

about abortion. I wanted to keep the baby, but well-meaning family members and friends said we were foolish to do so. They told us to consider all the possible problems, such as blindness or mental retardation, that the baby might have. My husband and I agonized.

At the time there were no support groups and we did not know much about abortion. There were no Right to Life Sundays, and people either advised us to "just start over" or admitted that they didn't know what to tell us. I turned to Psalms for comfort. I still have *The Living Bible* in which I underlined in pink all the verses that ministered to me during those hard weeks.

I pleaded with the Lord to tell us what to do. Should I keep the baby or have an abortion as I was being advised? I wrestled in prayer for twenty-one days. I felt like my prayers hit the ceiling and bounced back. Where was God? I wondered.

Finally, one day while kneeling at my bed and pouring out my heart to God, I very keenly sensed his presence and peace. I then heard the Lord speak to my heart. *Marilyn, you don't know what that baby is like, but I do. Trust Me.* It was so real! I knew it was not my own voice, because I experienced a great calm in my soul that had not been there before. I could not have manufactured that kind of instant peace.

The Lord did not promise us a healthy, normal baby that day, but he did promise that he would be with us no matter what that baby was like. His presence and the knowledge that he was in control were our sources of comfort and assurance. The Lord also comforted me with verses from Psalm 91: "We live within the shadow of the Almighty, sheltered by the God who is above all gods. . . . He will shield you with his wings! They will shelter you. His faithful promises are your armor" (vv. 1, 4, TLB). The Lord could have easily shielded our baby from all the radiation with his wings. I knew, however, that his faithful promise to be with us was what I needed most.

As the weeks passed, I continued to feel his peace. When I

was three months pregnant, I received a letter from my mother-in-law. Since my own mother had passed away when I was a young teen, I treasured my relationship with her. Receiving her letter made me smile.

"Heavenly Father," I said quietly, "it is so nice to get a letter from my mother-in-law. I wish I could also get a letter from my own mother. I would really like to talk to her about this pregnancy—it's just one of those mother-daughter type things."

After finishing my vacuuming, I sat down to rest on the stair step. My glance fell on a stack of letters. They had belonged to an aunt who had recently passed away. I had already been through the pile, but as I sat there I noticed a small envelope that I had missed the first time around. Inside the envelope was a baby announcement. When I opened it, I was surprised to see that it was *my* birth announcement! I had never seen mine before.

Wow, what fun timing, I thought.

As I gingerly held the card in my hand, I noticed that the card unfolded and that there was writing on the inside. It was a letter from my mother to my aunt. Memories washed over me as I saw her familiar handwriting. The letter spoke of my mother's difficult pregnancy with me. (She was forty-five at the time.) The doctor did not even expect her to live. He was not sure I was going to make it either. She mentions how the doctor prayed with her as she went into the delivery room. He asked the Lord to spare our lives. While my mother needed complete bed rest for two months following my birth, obviously he had allowed us to live.

Tears began to trickle down my cheeks. Here was a letter written by my mother about her difficult pregnancy. I had never heard that story. Somehow the Lord had saved that letter for twenty-three years until I, too, was in a difficult pregnancy! I felt like the Lord had answered my prayer and allowed me a "visit" with my mother. How great our God is!

The day came for our child's birth. When I got to the hospital, I was told that the baby had turned and was now breech. More X rays were needed. I remember saying to the Lord that there was nothing I could do about it, and that again he would have to shield this child with his wings.

I was anesthetized, so I did not know immediately about the baby's physical or mental health. A short time later, I awoke and the nurse placed a small pink bundle in my arms. "Is she okay?" I asked.

"She is perfectly whole," the nurse replied with a smile. Tears streamed down my cheeks.

Now choose life, so that you and your children may live and that you may love the Lord your God, listen to his voice, and hold fast to him.
Deuteronomy 30:19-20

The Lord had never said that the baby would be fine. He simply reassured me of his promise to help us no matter what happened. Looking back, I know the Lord spoke comfort and peace to my heart as I knelt by my bed so many years ago.

I had reasoned that the Lord had spoken like that because I faced a real crisis and because I had spent so much time in prayer. It had never occurred to me that God desired to speak to my heart that way in everyday matters.

One other listening incident from our seminary days stands out. We did not fully catch its significance until years later, however—perhaps because it did not occur during a major crisis. One evening, just as we were getting ready to sit down for dinner, I told Paul that we had no bread to make sandwiches for lunch the next day. We were on an extremely tight budget and had no money to buy a loaf.

"Maybe we will just have to eat spoonfuls of peanut butter," I said. "I don't know what else to pack for our lunch tomorrow." We sat down to eat our meager dinner.

Paul prayed for our meal and closed by asking, "Lord Jesus, we need some bread, and just like you taught your disciples to do, we ask you to please give us our daily bread." During dinner, some seminary friends called to ask if they could stop by about a half hour later.

When they arrived, the wife carried a tray with a white towel over it. The husband explained that his wife had recently learned how to bake bread and that the recipe she used made three loaves. "We decided that whenever she bakes bread we would keep one loaf and give the other two away. Well, we dropped off one of the loaves and then decided to take the other loaf to the president of the seminary. We drove over to his house, but he wasn't home. We were disappointed, but we decided to drive back home and ask God whom he wanted us to share this third loaf of bread with. When we asked him to put a name on our heart, your names came to our mind. We hope you don't mind."

At that point, the wife uncovered a loaf of wheat and molasses bread. For a moment Paul and I were speechless as we stared at the loaf of bread. "How did you know we needed bread?" I asked. "Paul just prayed that God would give us some bread so I could make sandwiches for our lunch tomorrow."

"We didn't know you needed bread," our friends replied, "but we clearly heard the Lord telling us to share a loaf with the Hontzes." Our friends had been concerned that they would offend us by sharing their bread with us. Nothing could have been further from the truth. Once they realized that we had prayed for bread and they had been the answer to that prayer, we were all ecstatic.

That night I was in awe of how God had answered our prayer for bread, though I did not yet grasp the remarkable truth that God desired to speak to me regularly, just as he had spoken to our friends.

LESSONS IN LISTENING

In the fall of 1993, however, everything I heard or read seemed to be about hearing God's voice. Listening to God was becoming a daily adventure, and I never knew where he was going to take me next. I felt as if I were on one of those amusement park rides that takes people on a wild course through a dark building. The riders have no idea what twists and turns are ahead. All they can do is hold on tight and enjoy the ride. The Lord desires me to hold on tight to him, to trust him as together we live one day at a time.

Without knowing about my new adventure in listening for God, my friend Marlae called and told me about a great book she'd read. It was written by Mary Geegh, a missionary to India who worked at a mission school for thirty-eight years. Her book, *God Guides,* influenced me tremendously as I learned what it means to listen to God. Mary deliberately took time to listen to the Lord and then wrote anything she sensed that he was saying to her. "I determined to listen to God for guidance in all matters," she wrote, "and I promised him I would obey whatever he told me. There were so many things that needed solutions."

She described the friction that existed between herself and a colleague. The coworker had ten children and was often ill, so many times she was unable to work. Mary felt this woman was unfairly trying to hold on to her job, while often leaving her work for others to do.

Early one morning Mary asked God for help in dissolving the critical feelings she felt toward this colleague.

The thought, *Take her a fresh egg,* came to Mary. "That wasn't my idea," wrote Mary, "and who would say that was guidance! A dozen fresh eggs might be reasonable—but one! That might insult my colleague. So, I wrote it off and gave up for that morning."

When Mary returned home from teaching her classes at the mission school, she discovered a chicken sitting in an armchair in her living room. The hen flew down, leaving behind a freshly laid egg! "That had never happened before, nor since," recalled Mary. "I remembered what I had scratched out in my new 'guidance' notebook: 'Take her a fresh egg.'"

Still Mary argued with God, afraid the colleague would laugh at her if she brought her the single egg. *Results are not your business,* she felt the Lord say. *Your business is obedience.*

Mary finally took the egg to her coworker's house. She was relieved to see one of the sons outside. She asked him to give the egg to his mother. Mary quickly left.

That evening the colleague asked why she had brought the egg. When Mary explained, the woman said, "That's just like God! He knew I had nothing to eat this day. There just wasn't enough food for all, so I went without. Then you brought the egg for me. When I ate it, I felt so satisfied and strengthened."[21]

From that point on, the woman also began to listen to God daily for guidance. Mary experienced a change as well: all the friction in her heart was gone, and for the first time she felt love and compassion toward the coworker and her family.

Mary Geegh was a living example of a woman who totally depended on the Lord for guidance and wisdom. I had the privilege of meeting her when she was ninety-four years old. She was still seeking to hear God speak to her! She lived another seven years and was my model of someone who actively listened for the voice of God.

HEARING GOD'S VOICE

One morning while I was seeking to understand this new way of being quiet before the Lord, the phone rang. A distraught college student was calling.

"You don't know me," she said, "but I am really struggling with a heavy problem. I'm leaving for home in a few minutes and someone suggested I call you."

As I listened to her, I knew I had no answers for her. In the quietness of my heart I prayed, *Father, please help me know what to say to this precious girl.*

I sensed the Lord softly impressing me to ask her a simple question: Had she told her mom about the problem? The question didn't make sense to me, because her mom was not a part of the problem. Finally, as the prompting became more urgent, I asked her.

There was silence. Quietly, she said, "You are the third person to ask me that same question. I'm on my way home now; I will talk to my mom about this."

Later she told me that while her mom was not at all a part of the problem, she turned out to be part of the solution. Her mom was the key that unlocked the pain that had held this girl captive.

I am so glad that the Lord was patient with me as I tried to learn more about listening to him. I was so unsure about this new territory, yet I started to see that the events occurring in my life were not coincidence or happenstance. God wanted to be specific about his guidance.

One other event in the fall of 1993 left me completely convinced that the Father did want me to listen to him. This one hit a little closer to home.

After attending Bible Study Fellowship at our church one morning, I ran up to see my husband in the church office. As soon as I saw his face, I knew something was wrong. He told me that there was a fifteen-hundred-dollar error in our checking account. We had never even had this much in our account, so it was a huge amount to us.

"The bank told me they will help us find out what happened, but in the meantime, Marilyn, do not write any checks." I said I wouldn't and then mentioned that I was on my way home and would spend some time in prayer concerning this matter.

"How are you going to pray?" asked my discouraged husband. "I suppose you're going to ask the Lord to send us a check for fifteen hundred dollars."

"No," I replied, "but I am going to pray that the bank will be able to find out what happened and that we will be good stewards of our resources to pay this large debt." I went straight to my prayer closet when I reached home.

As I finished praying I realized that I had intended to write a ten dollar check for our Wednesday night supper at church that evening. I had already told our children that we would meet at the church at five. One child was at soccer; another at track; and a third was at cheerleading. How would I get messages to them?

I know this is a very small thing, Father, I prayed, *but would you somehow make it possible for all of us to get to church supper tonight and then provide ten dollars for us?* As soon as I finished praying, I remembered I had put away a ten-dollar bill in a kitchen cupboard to start my Christmas gift fund. "Thanks, Lord," I said out loud, "I forgot about that money, and it will help us out for tonight."

As I stood in line to pay the cashier that evening, he mentioned that someone had already paid for our church supper. "Who paid?" I asked incredulously.

"I can't tell you," he replied with a smile. "The person wants to remain anonymous." I was taken aback. We had been going to church suppers at this church for seventeen years. No one had ever paid for our church supper before (and no one has since)!

It dawned on me that if God could take care of a ten-dollar need, he could care for a huge fifteen-hundred-dollar need. Tears welled up in my eyes while I carried our tray of food to a table. A deep sense of peace washed over me as I again realized that God cares about and provides for every part of our lives.

Ten days later, we received an express mail delivery envelope. Inside were two small envelopes. I opened one of them and gasped. I was holding a check for fifteen hundred dollars! Shaking, I quickly opened the other small envelope, which contained a note from the people who had sent the check. It said, "Do not think of this as a gift from us, but from God." I could not believe my eyes. I looked again at the return address. These people lived far away, were not relatives, and had no idea that we had a financial need. In fact, we had told no one about it.

I enjoyed the conversation I had with my husband that evening. "Honey," I began, "remember how you have teased me about praying for a fifteen-hundred-dollar check?"

Paul nodded and looked at me.

"Well, it arrived today."

"No," my husband said, laughing.

"Yes, it did!" I exclaimed jubilantly.

"No," he countered again.

"Yes, Paul, it did come today."

As the kids shouted, "Show him the check, Mom!" I pulled it out from behind my back.

Paul said, "Only the Lord could have done this. We need to thank him." In a joyous spirit we all knelt down beside our blue couch and offered praise and thanksgiving to the Lord.

Later that evening I called the people who had sent us the check. I thanked them profusely for their wonderful and timely gift. Without telling them our story, I asked them, "Why did you send the amount that you did? Why not ten dollars or one hundred dollars? Even that would have been so generous."

I will never forget their reply. They explained that the morning before we received their envelope, they each had been in their own quiet time. When they finished praying, one told the other of getting the sense that Paul and Marilyn Hontz had a financial need. The other had sensed the same thing. They went back to prayer and individually asked the Lord to confirm an amount to them. When they came back together, they had the same amount in mind—fifteen hundred dollars.

Now, I have to tell you that as wonderful as it was to receive that check, the bigger miracle to me was learning that two people had heard God's voice and then had obeyed his prompting! I wanted to live like that. You can too. The question is, will we pay attention?

CHAPTER 11

Does God Speak to His Children?

*R*emember the Magic 8 Ball? It's a black plastic ball with a twenty-sided answer cube floating in the murky water inside it. Invented in the 1940s, it was initially promoted as an interesting conversation piece or a trendy paperweight. Unfortunately, some people began to use it to try and discern easy answers to life's difficult questions.

Listening for God's voice should *never* be seen as akin to playing with a toy that you shake until the answer you want pops up. God is not a genie who does what you want if you rub him just right.

Neither should we listen to God so that we may say to others, "God told me to tell you" or "God told me to, so I can do what I want to do." How we must sadden our heavenly Father when we do this. I never like it when someone puts words in my mouth, yet that's the very thing we can do to the Lord Jesus.

Listening to God is not seeking "inside information," but rather seeking guidance to do God's will. (And not just during a crisis time either!) It is a time to get *his* perspective and peace on a matter and to truly hear what he would like done. This intimate relationship develops as we seek the Lord through prevailing prayer and diligent reading of his Word.

Perhaps you're thinking, *But I've never heard God speak to me before.* Do you know that if you have invited Jesus into your life, God has already spoken personally to you? It was at his invitation that you became his child. First Peter 2:9 says that God has "called you out of darkness into his wonderful light." You heard his call and responded.

Scripture makes it clear that as we seek to follow the Lord and obey him, he will communicate with us. Psalm 25:14 says, "The Lord confides in those who fear him." Proverbs 3:32 is similar: He "takes the upright into his confidence."

Christ desires to resume fellowship even with those Christians who have fallen into sin and stopped listening for his voice. Revelation 3:19-20 presents a vivid picture of Jesus standing at the heart's door of one of his wayward followers. He says, "I am the one who corrects and disciplines everyone I love. Be diligent and turn from your indifference. Look! Here I stand at the door and knock. If you hear me calling and open the door, I will come in, and we will share a meal as friends" (NLT).

Do you belong to God? Have you turned your life over to Christ? If you are pursuing your own way, are you willing to confess your sins and invite Jesus to fellowship with you? If so, you can hear what he says. John 8:47 clearly states: "He who belongs to God hears what God says." Does God really speak to his children? The answer is a resounding yes!

Another thing I have learned is that God does not have favorites. Listening is for every child of God—you do not have to be a seasoned saint. John Ortberg says in his book *The Life*

You've Always Wanted, "Hearing God speak to us is no indication that we are unusually spiritual or mature or important. God is able to communicate with whomever He chooses."[22]

WHAT THE WORD SAYS ABOUT LISTENING

John 10:27 says, "My sheep listen to my voice; I know them, and they follow me." Are you one of God's sheep? Are you listening to his voice?

If you have been a Christian for a while, you have probably discovered that your thoughts and ways are *not* the same as God's (see Isaiah 55:8). Yet Amos 4:13 tells us that God "reveals his thoughts to man." That is incredible! We don't deserve it, but he delights to reveal himself to us. He gives us his mind and his thoughts. "Strange as it seems, we Christians actually do have within us a portion of the very thoughts and mind of Christ" (1 Corinthians 2:16, TLB). But too often we opt to follow our own thoughts. We forget that the Lord is willing and ready to share his thoughts with us. Ask him, seek him, and keep knocking. He will respond to you.

So what does listening look like? We find a beautiful visual aid in Luke 10:39, in which Mary "sat at the Lord's feet listening to what he said." Can't you just picture her sitting there at the feet of Jesus—one woman surrounded by all those men? I, too, want to be found sitting, listening to him.

Even Jesus modeled listening when he paused to talk with his Father during his earthly ministry. Consider how he spent the night just before calling the twelve apostles: "Jesus went to a mountain to pray, and he prayed to God all night. At daybreak he called together all of his disciples and chose twelve of them to be apostles" (Luke 6:12-13, NLT). How did he know which of his many followers to choose to become part of his inner circle? His Father told him.

Jesus also said, "I do nothing on my own but speak just what the Father has taught me" (John 8:28). He said in John

6:45, "Everyone who listens to the Father and learns from him comes to me."

One of our dogs, a small, white, fluffy mix named Maggie, adored our daughter Mandy. Exactly twenty minutes before Mandy was due home from high school, Maggie would position herself at the front door and wait patiently for Mandy to walk in. Maggie's nose was always pointed toward that door; no one could distract her. I used to laugh and say, "Oh, Maggie, who told you it was time to wait for Mandy?"

The writer of Proverbs 8:34 might have had a loyal dog in mind when he wrote, "Blessed is the man who listens to me, watching daily at my doors, waiting at my doorway." Do I wait and listen for the Lord like this? I want to.

We are commanded to "be still, and know that I am God" (Psalm 46:10). Even when we are still before the Lord and do not hear anything from him, it is not wasted time. To reflect on him and to know that he is God is very productive.

But are you familiar with the rest of Psalm 46:10? It concludes: "I will be exalted among the nations, I will be exalted in the earth." I'd like to think that as we quiet ourselves before the Lord and listen, it not only blesses us but the world as well. When we listen, God can put on our hearts how to reach out to our neighbor or anyone else in the world.

WHY GOD WANTS TO SPEAK TO YOU

God wants to be intimate with you

God's eternal being is a tri-unity: a love relationship between the Father, Son, and Holy Spirit. In fact, God was already in this intimate relationship before he created us. Since God's very nature is to be relational, and we are made in his image, we must conclude that we too are created for relationship.

We humans are the only creatures God made with mouths that speak! He created us to have a personal relationship with him—to commune with him and to listen to him. God wants us to know him. He wants to be known by us.

God wants to communicate his love to you

God calls us the bride of Christ—obviously he feels great love and affection for his church. I'm reminded of the old story about the wife who asks her husband, "Why don't you tell me you love me anymore?" The husband replies, "I told you on our wedding day that I loved you. If anything changes, I'll let you know."

God is not like that. Every day the Lord whispers his love to us. "I belong to my lover, and his desire is for me" (Song of Songs 7:10). His desire is for you!

God brings Scriptures to our mind to encourage and comfort us. God wants our heart and mind to be convinced of the passionate love he has for us. He wants us to feel treasured and cherished by him. You are God's personal concern.

God desires to guide you

The Lord also wishes to guide, correct, and encourage us. Just this morning I laid out a request to the Lord that may seem petty to others but was important to me. I was asked (along with others) to write a tribute for an outstanding woman in our community. I agreed to do so, but absolutely nothing came to my mind. She definitely deserved the tribute; it's just that I did not know what to write. I needed the Lord's creativity.

As I prayed and then listened, the Lord gave me the answer for that project, as well as Scripture to include. I sensed such joy and peace as I realized that the Lord had imparted his creativity to me. I've learned that God wants to guide us even more than we want him to. He delights when we ask, in the same way parents love to have a child ask for their advice.

God wants to let you in on his agenda

God does not want to hide his will from us. He wants us to ask him for his agenda for our lives. Psalm 139:16 says, "You saw me before I was born and scheduled each day of my life before I began to breathe. Every day was recorded in your Book!" (TLB). He has a purpose—an agenda—for you, and it was in place before you took your first breath.

Most mornings I plan out my day on a to-do list and cross off items as they are accomplished. The Lord challenged me one morning to make room on my page for *his* to-do list. I remember saying, *Oh, Father, it's so easy for me to know my agenda for the day, but I never thought about asking for your agenda.*

Now, every morning when I write my list, I listen to see if God wants me to do something for him. This morning as I listened, the Holy Spirit brought five people and their situations to my thoughts. They were all people I needed to write, call, or e-mail. I had not even been thinking about these people! The Father will gladly share his agenda with us if we ask and then listen.

God wants you to intercede for others

Another reason God desires to speak to us is so that we may know when and how to pray for someone. Have you ever awakened in the night with someone's name on your mind? Or have you ever sensed an urgency to pray for someone as you were going about a typical day? That may have been the Lord alerting you to pray. Many missionaries have found that some-one was praying for them at the exact time they faced a crisis.

This past January 5, I was asking God whether or not I should consider writing a book. Often when I spoke at confer-ences and retreats I was asked if I had written any books. I had to tell them no. One day our local bookstore called and asked if I had books because they had some calls requesting them. I laughed and again said no. *Was the Lord trying to tell me some-thing?* I wondered. I knew I was not a writer, yet the requests kept coming. I decided to ask my daughter Christy to join me in prayer about this "writing thing." As we prayed, I sensed God's peace. I knew that he had heard my request and would guide me in the coming months.

> *He who belongs to God hears what God says.*
>
> **Jesus, in John 8:47**

Two weeks later, I received a card in the mail from a woman named Judy who attends our church. This godly lady was writing to tell me that she had been prompted to pray for me. At one point she mentioned that she had been led to pray for "Marilyn and a book," but she had no idea what that meant. She hoped I would know. It was the very thing Christy and I had prayed about! This woman would not have known about this matter—only my daughter knew the need. I looked at the envelope and noticed the postmark date: January 5!

A few weeks later, after I had gotten over my amazement that Judy "knew," I called her and thanked her for her letter. I then told her that the matter she had been prompted to pray about was the very thing my daughter and I had been praying for. She was amazed too. She then told me her side of the story. She had felt prompted to pray for me, but the prompting did not make sense to her. She wrote the note but decided not to send it. She changed her mind again and decided to mail it. Fearing that she would seem weird for following this prompting, however, she took her letter out of the mailbox. When the prompting continued, she told the Lord that if the mailman had not come yet she would go ahead and mail it. Because the mailman almost always came at the same time—and that time had passed—she was certain he had already been there. When she went out again to her mailbox, she saw that he had not yet arrived. Feeling rather foolish, she finally put the letter out for him to pick up.

"Marilyn," she said, "I cannot tell you how encouraging it is to hear that my note made sense to you. That has never happened to me before. I was really down in the dumps this morning, pouring out my heart to the Lord about my sons who do not know the Lord. I asked him to encourage me. I said, *Lord, do you even hear me when I pray? Are you listening to me?*

"Now, you are calling to say that God answered your prayer through my letter. He really does hear and answer prayer, doesn't he? This encourages me to keep on praying for my grown sons to come to Christ."

It was no accident that I called the day I did. I found out that it was the anniversary date of the death of her husband, and she had been crying just before I called. Only the Holy Spirit could have revealed to her how she should pray for me. And only he could prompt me to call to thank her on the very day that she most needed encouragement. Many times I have seen how listening after interceding for others not only benefits the listener but blesses other people as well.

WHY YOU SHOULD LISTEN

Listening is a command from God

When Jesus was transfigured before three of his disciples, the Father said, "This is my Son, whom I love. Listen to him!" (Mark 9:7). God still desires a two-way conversation with us. Prayer is the time we talk to him; listening is the time we give to the Lord to talk to us.

When we are quiet and allow the Lord to have access to our hearts, he replaces our me-focused attitudes with Christ-focused ones.

Listening gives the Holy Spirit an opportunity to share what is on his heart

At one time, I spent all of my prayer time pouring out my thoughts to the Lord without giving him an opportunity to speak.

He used a visit to our pediatrician to help me understand

why I needed to listen as well. I had taken Abby to the doctor and explained to him that she had an earache, swollen glands, a sore throat, and a fever. The doctor made his diagnosis and prescribed medication.

As we went out the door, the Lord asked me, *What if you took Abby into the examining room, explained her symptoms to the doctor, and then left without waiting for a diagnosis?* It was as if the Lord was saying to me that I was coming to him with all my "symptoms" (which was a good start), but that I walked out of the prayer closet door before finding out his diagnosis or "prescription" for the problem. I needed to wait for the Lord and not rush out of my prayer time. This listening time is critical. It is when our Great Physician has an opportunity to speak to our hearts and minds and tell us what he would like to say.

Listening is essential when we are involved in kingdom work

Many times people tell me about their heartbreaking losses, and I don't know what to say. So often the Lord brings to my mind just the right verse or the right words. Recently I felt prompted to write a note to a woman from our congregation who was going through a tough time. I asked the Lord to show me the exact Scripture verse for her. I felt led to include a verse from Psalms in my note. I saw her a few weeks later, and she told me how encouraging my note had been. "That verse you chose, especially, was perfect. How did you know?" she asked.

I really didn't know; it was the Holy Spirit who led me to it.

My husband and I have served at the same church for the last twenty-seven years. We have had many wonderful times, but we have had some difficult times as well. This past spring was a discouraging time. We sought God on this matter through prayer and fasting. Our hearts were grieving and we did not know what to do.

Then in early March we received a devastating letter. We never mind when anyone shares his or her opinion with us, but this letter did not extend grace in any way. It was harsh and extremely critical. After reading the letter, I held it up to the Lord and cried out for mercy.

Lord Jesus, please show us any truth in this letter. (We have learned that many times there are nuggets of truth in critical letters, and we want to have teachable spirits.) I laid my hands on the letter and prayed again. *Father, please give us wisdom to know how to respond to these people. Help us, too, to take to heart what we need to hear, and then to "blow away" anything that is just chaff.*

I wrestled for days over this letter! Satan had used his tool of discouragement to pry open my heart. I realized I had become depressed.

Finally, lying facedown on the floor in my prayer closet, I cried out in desperation to God. All I could do was ask him to be merciful to us and show us what to do. After lying there quite a while, I sat up and reached for my Bible. I began to read from Mark 10. The passage was about a blind man by the name of Bartimaeus. He heard that Jesus was going to walk past where he was sitting. He wanted to be healed, so he cried out to Jesus for healing mercy.

Some of the people told him to be quiet. After all, who did Bartimaeus think he was? But Jesus noticed Bartimaeus and called for him. Interestingly the crowd around Bartimaeus changed its tune once they knew he was important to Jesus.

Someone in the crowd said to Bartimaeus, "Cheer up! On your feet. He's calling you." (Mark 10:49). As I read that verse, I felt as if God had highlighted it with a bright yellow marker just for me! The Lord whispered in a very tender way to my weary heart: *Marilyn, cheer up.* He didn't say it as if he were disgusted with me; instead, I sensed it was a gentle calling to cheer up because Jesus was coming my way. He had noticed me in my condition. I was to get up on my feet and he would help pull me up. He knew I felt as if I were in a pit so slippery that I could not climb out of it alone.

The Lord also used the statement "He's calling you" to remind me that *he* is the one who calls me. My sense of calling for ministry had been shattered. He was restoring the call once again. The Word of God spoke directly to me! I clung to that verse and meditated on it over and over.

Later that day, my mentor, Kathleen, called. Normally when she calls we chitchat a bit and then talk about what God is doing in our lives. This phone call was different. Though I had not told her what I was going through, Kathleen began by saying, "Marilyn, I need to tell you that I sensed a burden to pray for you beginning yesterday afternoon. I continued to feel prompted to pray for you during the night. This morning I again felt the need to lift you in prayer."

She said that she finally asked the Lord why I was so much on her mind. She then said, "You are in a low-grade depression." I gasped because I had not told anyone. I had been able to cover my sadness with my friends. I thought it wouldn't be good for people in the congregation to know that their pastor's wife was secretly fighting depression. I was wrong! I am so glad the Lord revealed what was behind my mask to my friend. I needed help and was too embarrassed to ask for it.

Kathleen told me I needed to make an appointment with my physician and offered some other suggestions for dealing with the depression. She ended up greatly encouraging me. I could not get over the timing of her call or her discernment. She had been listening to the Lord's prompting and obediently called me. Kathleen's call made a marked difference in my life.

The next afternoon, I went to a retreat center to spend time listening to the Lord. I asked God to continue the healing process that he had begun through the Word and through my mentor. As I was quiet before him, I clearly heard his voice speak to me.

Marilyn, you can either allow the church situation to drain *you or to* train *you.* It hit me hard! I had to make a choice in this matter. Could I trust the Lord to do something good through this painful situation? At that point, waves of relinquishment washed over me. "Father," I whispered, "I already know that this situation can drain me. Now if you can use it to train me, then go for it. There is no one else I would rather be trained by than you."

Looking back, I saw how the Lord used a combination of his Word, prayer, and listening to ease my struggle. A great reason for listening to the Lord is the wonderful healing that he can bring to our heart and mind.

CHAPTER 12

How Does God Speak to His Children?

*W*hen our daughter Mandy was in high school, she underwent what was supposed to be a simple medical procedure. It ended up being a nightmare for her because a small nerve in her back was accidentally severed. Mandy went from being my joyful, party-waiting-to-happen daughter to a very depressed teen. She was in chronic back pain that robbed her of her vitality. Many months into the pain, Mandy asked me, "Mom, do you think I have this back pain because of some sin in my life?"

My heart sank. I immediately wanted to say, "Oh no, Mandy, that's not true for you at all." Mandy was the kind of kid any parent wants to have: fun-loving, always able to get the family laughing whenever we were tense. Her relationship with Jesus was real and vibrant.

I quickly asked the Lord to give me wisdom in knowing how to answer her. "Mandy," I replied, "that is a question I would like you to ask the Lord."

She said okay and went to her room. She stayed there for

MARILYN HONTZ

quite a while. Some time later she came downstairs to the kitchen and said, "Mom, I believe the Lord spoke to me about my question, and he gave me his answer."

"What's that, honey?" I asked.

"This is what I heard as I listened to him. He told me that he could heal me in an instant if he wanted to. But, Mom, for some reason he does not want to right now. Instead he wants to teach me something and I don't want to miss it."

Wow. I could have tried to tell her the same thing, but when she heard it from her heavenly Father, it ministered to her in a very powerful way. During the nine months it took for her damaged nerve to grow back, the Lord helped her to be more sensitive to others who are going through painful situations or who are depressed. She said that she could identify with the psalmist who wrote that "the darkness is my closest friend" (Psalm 88:18).

LEARNING TO LISTEN

Perhaps you are thinking, *Okay, this is great for you, but God just doesn't speak to me like he does to you or Mandy.* You know what? You're right. God doesn't speak to any of us in the same way. As our Creator, he communicates in ways that are unique to the way he made us. Here are some guidelines I found helpful in training my ears to hear his voice.

1. First of all, remind yourself that there is no set formula! The Holy Spirit will teach you as you seek to listen to him. I found that I had to *learn* to listen. Listening is not a skill you inherit; it has to be developed. I was encouraged to read that, as a young boy, the Old Testament prophet Samuel did not know that the Lord was speaking to him when he heard a voice in the night. However, after the third time, Eli the prophet helped Samuel realize the Lord was calling him (1 Samuel 3). (This story also reminds us how appropriate it is to teach our children to listen to the Lord.)

Just as God works uniquely in the lives of each of his children, so he speaks to them individually. In fact, the word *you* shows up several times in two of my favorite "guidance" verses. Isaiah 48:17 says: "I am the Lord your God, who teaches *you* what is best for *you,* who directs *you* in the way *you* should go." Psalm 32:8 says: "I will instruct *you* and teach *you* in the way *you* should go; I will counsel *you* and watch over *you*" (italics in both verses are mine). God is so personal!

2. *Remember to ask for a clean heart. An impure heart muffles God's voice.* Proverbs 1:23 states: "If you had responded to my rebuke, I would have poured out my heart to you and made my thoughts known to you." Ask the Lord if there is any sin in your life that needs to be cleared up. Is there an attitude that needs to be adjusted?

3. *Believe that God does speak and will speak to you if you ask him to do so.* Unbelief can keep a person from hearing God. If you struggle with this, ask the Lord to help your unbelief (Mark 9:24). Meditate on Scriptures that tell us that he speaks, such as: "Long ago God spoke many times and in many ways to our ancestors through the prophets. But now in these final days, he has spoken to us through his Son" (Hebrews 1:1-2, NLT) Next, ask him to speak to your heart as you read the Word.

4. *One of the best ways to practice listening is to read the Bible until the Lord speaks to you.* Say to the Lord, "What is it you want me to hear today from your Word?" The Lord will personalize his Scripture to you, and it will be just what you need for that day.

Today as I was reading the third chapter of Hebrews a phrase from one of the verses caught my attention: "Fix your thoughts on Jesus" (v. 1). Those words keep coming to my heart. It has been a great reminder for me to keep focused on the Lord in the middle of all that I'm trying to accomplish today.

5. *Take time to listen quietly after you read the Word and after you pray.* One morning I read, "He who guards his mouth and his tongue keeps himself from calamity" (Proverbs 21:23). After that I turned to Psalm 51, my other reading for the day. I couldn't help

noticing how verse 15 tied in with the Proverbs verse: "O Lord, open my lips, and my mouth will declare your praise."

After I read those verses and prayed, I sensed the Lord speaking to my own heart (again) about eliminating critical or negative words from my conversations. I found it interesting that the first verse reminded me to guard my mouth to keep me from calamity, and the second gave a good and productive alternative for my mouth—to praise the Lord.

As I listened in silence, I heard the Lord say, *Marilyn, today is your fast day. Would you be willing to try a fast from criticalness?*

Father, I replied, *I've tried that before, and I only made it through about ten minutes of the day.*

The Lord continued to speak to my heart: *What about asking me to stop you before you say anything negative—about others or yourself—and instead letting me open your mouth so that your lips declare my praise?*

On this day my adult children were home, my younger son had three friends over, my husband was home on a vacation day, and I was surrounded by three barking dogs—lots of causes for calamity. I had a lot of praising to do that day!

Guess what? I blew it. But I'm a bit further along on my spiritual journey. I'm a bit more in tune to this area in which the Holy Spirit wants to help me. I'm also aware of some of my hidden heart issues that need to be addressed. I didn't see them before and can no longer ignore this blind spot. How great that the Lord loves me too much to let me continue in an unhealthy pattern. Much is gained by taking time to listen after Bible reading and prayer. At times it may seem risky, but it is worth it.

6. Don't be sidetracked by distractions. If you often feel distracted as you try to listen, it is okay. If you remember you need to do something (such as pick up the suit at the dry cleaners, start the dishwasher, or mow the lawn), write it down on a piece of paper to deal with it later. Sometimes a name or situation may pop into your mind and you wonder, *Where did that* come from? The Lord could be bringing that name to you in those quiet moments. Again, jot down the name and deal with it when you are through listening.

Remember that sometimes a distraction can be a good thing. Perhaps it is yet another way the Lord is prompting you to connect with someone. I appreciate what St. Francis of Assisi said: "If your heart wanders or is distracted, bring it back and replace it tenderly in the presence of the Master. Even if you have to do this all hour—your hour would still be well employed."

7. As you listen, ask the Lord questions. For example: *Whom do you want me to pray for? Is there something you would like to reveal to me about my own heart? Is there someone you want me to send an encouraging note to? Lord Jesus, what do you want me to do today that will make a difference for eternity?* Such questions are a great way to begin your day of listening to God.

8. Write down or journal what you sense God is prompting you to do. Recently I talked to the Lord about a fear of failure I had. After I prayed, I sat and listened with a pen in hand. The Lord reminded me of a question he once asked Moses: "Is the Lord's arm too short?" (Numbers 11:23). Next came the phrase from Job "no plan of [God's] can be thwarted" (42:2). Then I sensed this question: *Marilyn, have I ever proved to be inadequate to meet your needs?*

No, Father. I know that you are able to meet all my needs.

Then believe what you know, he told me. God was asking me to trust in his strength. That was my guidance for the day. About an hour later I received an encouraging e-mail from someone about the very thing I had felt so inadequate about.

9. As you listen, wait for God's confirmation through the Word and other people. I have found that the Lord usually confirms his guidance. While Mandy was suffering from the severed nerve in her back, she discovered that her friends didn't know how to reach out to someone in constant pain. As a result, she felt lonely.

One morning I read a verse that I sensed I was to share with her. "Let your gentleness be evident to all. The Lord is near" (Philippians 4:5). *Mandy lives out that verse; she is gentle,* whispered that still, small voice. Mandy has a sweet spirit, and it takes quite a bit to ruffle her feathers; however, she was discouraged from the physical and emotional pain. I wrote the verse on a sticky note and attached it to her bathroom mirror, hoping it would encourage her. I added a note saying that her gentleness was evident to all and reminding her that the Lord was near to her.

Later that day she thanked me for the verse. "That verse makes me want to be more gentle. I want to try to live up to what it says." I believe it is important to encourage your child when you see character traits that are godly, and I wanted Mandy to know that I had seen the fruit of the Spirit displayed in her.

That evening our family was invited to a party where we knew very few people. Toward the end of the party, a lady we had just met came up to us. Turning to Mandy she said, "I have been watching you all evening as you went around talking with both the adults and the children. You have such a gentle spirit." Mandy and I looked at each other and smiled. There was that word again—gentle.

"You see," I later said to Mandy, "very often when the Lord wants us to hear something from him, he will confirm it through others." This was a great encouragement to her.

10. Be prepared to obey what the Lord prompts you to do. It is important to respond with obedience to what you hear. God may not give you more guidance until you obey what he has already told you to do. If the Lord prompts me to call someone, but I put it off, he may remind me again. If I still do not obey, the prompting eventually fades. If you know that you have ignored the Spirit's leading, ask him to forgive you and keep listening for his voice.

11. Ask the Lord to train you to listen for his still, small voice throughout your day. I love how the Lord can interrupt our day with his prompting even when we are caught up in other activities. Remember, listening doesn't only happen when you are quiet.

My daughter Holly recently gave me a wonderful illustration of listening throughout our day. She said, "Mom, you know how we can be in the same room together but be busy with different things? Well, even though we are busy and not engaged in conversation, our ears immediately perk up if one of us starts to speak." So true. We can be busy, yet alert. Jesus is always in the same room with us. Do your ears perk up when he speaks—even when you're in the middle of a project?

12. Thank the Lord that he will speak to you in his way and his timing. The Word says that he will answer in the time of his favor (Isaiah 49:8). Sitting silently at the Master's feet is *never* wasted time. Even if you hear nothing from the Lord Jesus, just sitting and basking in his presence is an awesome experience.

Once you begin to spend time each day listening for God's voice, consider devoting an extended period of time with him. Just as Jesus often retreated from the crowds to draw strength from his Father, so you can be reinvigorated by occasionally removing yourself from normal daily routines. See appendix C for some ideas on how you might plan this time alone with God.

HOW DOES GOD SPEAK?

I believe the Lord speaks to his children today in four different ways.

The Word of God

The number one way God guides us is through his Word, the Bible. Whatever we believe we hear from the Lord must align with his written Word. We do not read the Bible expecting to find new revelations. No, we read it for the Lord to tell us how to personally apply what he has already said in his Word. The Word of God is our primary source of guidance!

The Holy Spirit

The Holy Spirit can and will speak to our heart in quiet ways. Sometimes he will bring a Scripture to your remembrance. At other times he will remind you to pray for someone. Often he will use an "inner impression" or a prompting to catch your attention. Once you begin to recognize his voice, there can be no doubt who is speaking. Acts 17:28 says, "For in him we live and move and have our being."

It is no wonder that we are able to hear those impressions from the Holy Spirit—as long as we are keeping in step with him. "Since we live by the Spirit, let us keep in step with the Spirit" (Galatians 5:25).

The Holy Spirit is our Teacher who guides us in all things. John 14:26 says, "But the Counselor, the Holy Spirit, whom the Father will send in my name, will teach you all things and will remind you of everything I have said to you."

The godly counsel of others

God, at times, speaks through the advice of godly friends. Several years ago my husband and I were asked by our denomination to pray about leaving our church and starting a church in Germany. We prayed and prayed. We then asked thirty of our praying friends to pray with us about this opportunity. We arranged a time and place to meet after some days of prayer. When we all came together, we found that there was a unanimous thought. We were to stay where we were. It confirmed the peace that my husband and I had sensed about this decision.

Our circumstances

At times the Lord speaks through what is going on around you. Such guidance is not happenstance or coincidence. These are God-ordained, divine appointments.

I once drove my daughter Abby to an art class and, rather than waiting in the car, I decided to sit in on the session. Little did I know that the Lord was going to use that class to confirm some things in my life. As the instructor heated a glass rod and made it into a bead, she turned to me and began talking about an area of her life that God was dealing with. She immediately got my attention because it was the same area that the Lord had been impressing on me. We talked a bit, and then she handed me a book (that she "just happened" to have) about the very subject. As I left her work-shop that day, I realized that I wasn't there just to wait for Abby. The Lord wanted me there so he could confirm his direction during that art class.

> *A voice came from the cloud, saying, "This is my Son, whom I have chosen; listen to him."*
>
> **Luke 9:35**

Let me add, however, that I never rely *just* on the counsel of others, nor look at my circumstances as a sole source of guidance. I must first seek the Lord's counsel by reading the Word and spending much time in prayer. I am learning that I must always go to the best help, the Lord Jesus and his Word, before I go to the best of human help. If we seek him first in any given situation, he will make sure that we have the confirmation we need, which sometimes includes the godly counsel of others or our circumstances.

DISCERNING THE VOICES

Often people ask me, "How do you know it is the Lord speaking to you?" I wish I could point to a passage of Scripture that gave us a simple answer. While I can't do that, my own experience and those of others have convinced me that we can discern the source of the voices we hear. I believe we hear basically three voices: the voice of the Lord, the voice of self, and the voice of our enemy, Satan.

The voice of the Lord

Psalm 29:4 says that "the voice of the Lord is powerful; the voice of the Lord is majestic." From my own experience, I've found that the Lord's voice is a beautiful blend of gentleness and power. It speaks complete honesty and truth. God has the ability to speak to the depths of your soul, bringing profound peace and joy.

A sweetness prevails even when he is pointing out a wrong. His voice will seek to help you correct your behavior, yet he will never condemn your worth. God's voice tells you specifically what you need to confess. His guidance is always consistent with his Word and his holy character.

God's voice never contradicts Scripture. He will never make you rush into a major decision. He will lead you and allow you time to pray over matters so you can seek his will concerning decisions. Many times the Lord will whisper your name and tell you that he loves you. I believe the Lord Jesus wants you to understand that he loves you from "everlasting to everlasting" (Psalm103:17). His voice will always communicate a love that draws you to him.

The voice of self

The voice of self is recognizable by its selfish requests or desires. Our own voice is full of self-pity and self-righteousness. It wants to gratify fleshly desires.

Sometimes we go to the Lord and ask him to tell us things that we do not need to know. We must be on guard for wrong motives when we ask the Lord something. It is possible to say that we heard the Lord when really it was our own selfish desires clamoring for our attention. Our desires can be very strong! The Word tells us to "lean not on your own understanding" (Proverbs 3:5). Psalm 94:11 reminds us that "the Lord knows the thoughts of man; he knows that they are futile."

A woman once told me that she wanted to move to another house, so she prayed about it. She said that God told her to move and she did. The outcome was disastrous! She told me that she would never listen to God again. I questioned her a bit and learned that her desire to move had been very strong. She had not waited on the Lord in prayer, she had not sought his Word, and she had not waited on his timing.

Is God interested in where we live? Of course! It's just that the voice of self can be so loud that it drowns out the voice of the Lord. To guard against mistaking my voice for his, I must ask the Lord to silence the voice of self and to help me love him above every person, place, or material thing that I want.

The voice of the enemy

Satan's voice is cunning, negative, and critical. His voice will bring up past sins that you have already confessed and repented to the Lord. He will *condemn* you, whereas the Holy Spirit's voice will *convict* you. Satan can make you feel guilty or shameful, but you won't be able to specifically identify the cause of your feelings. The Spirit of the Lord, on the other hand, hones in on an area in your life and shows you a specific way to get rid of the guilt.

Unlike the Lord, Satan will try to push you to act on matters quickly. He will make you think that you have to make an immediate decision and that there is no time to pray about the situation.

He will also make you doubt your own worth. Have you ever found yourself saying "I can't do this" or "I am not intelligent enough" or "I'm so ugly"? I believe that Satan sometimes uses the "first person voice" to tell us something. If someone came up to you and said, "You are so ugly," you might get angry and try to defend yourself. If, however, you are standing in front of the mirror and all of a sudden *you* say, "I'm so fat" or "I'm so dumb," you're not likely to fight that. If you have a lot of negative self-talk, it could be the voice of your enemy seeking to destroy you.

Satan will also try to use Scripture out of context. (Look at cults for examples of this.) A man actually informed me that "God told him" to divorce his wife, leave their two children, and marry another woman. He believed that God and Scripture had confirmed his decision! Why did he think God had told him to divorce his wife? So that he and his new wife could be mission-aries. That may sound absurd, but the man was dead serious—and, of course, dead wrong. He did leave his wife and children to marry the other woman. No, they are not missionaries, and their life is full of struggles. They are reaping the consequences of listening to the enemy.

I have found it helpful to ask the Lord to silence any voice that is not the Lord's. It is also important to know the Word of God to help us distinguish between God's voice, our own voice, and the voice of the evil one. Remember God's voice will never contradict Scripture.

By the way, when Jesus was tempted in the desert, he had a weapon to fight Satan—the memorized Word of God. He didn't have a scroll to unroll and read. He knew the Scriptures by memory. This is a key to listening to God!

WHAT GETS IN OUR WAY

In addition to discerning the three different voices, we must also pull down any barriers *we* have put up that block our listening to the Lord.

Busyness and hurrying

The number one reason we do not hear the Lord speak is because we are too busy to take time to listen. I have found that the times I am really busy are the times I need him the most. It is hard to choose to neglect something else to take time to dwell on him. It's easier to give God our leftover time, rather than our best time.

A second reason, which is not far behind the first, is that we constantly rush through life. I often find myself saying, "I need to hurry and do this first before I spend time with the Lord."

We want everything in a hurry. I want my computer and microwave to hurry, and they were invented to hurry in the first place! *Hurry* is part of my daily vocabulary. I am so grateful that the Lord is never too busy or too hurried to respond to me.

Scripture reminds us to wait. "Be still in the presence of the Lord, and wait patiently for him to act" (Psalm 37:7, NLT). I think of Simeon, whom the Holy Spirit promised would see Jesus, the Messiah, before he died. By the time Mary and Joseph brought baby Jesus to the temple, Simeon was an old man. Yet listening and waiting had paid off for Simeon. (See Luke 2:25-35.)

Poor self-worth

A poor self-worth can hinder us from listening to God. We say to ourselves, *Why would God want to talk to me? I'm just a nobody. I have a bad past; I'm not good enough.* Moses is an example of someone who had poor self-worth. God actually spoke to him through a burning bush and asked him to help lead the Israelites out of bondage in Egypt. One would think that being called by God from a burning bush would have given him confidence that the Lord would help him with the task. Instead, look how Moses responded to God:

1. "Who am I to appear before Pharaoh?" (Exodus 3:11, NLT)
2. "If I go to the people of Israel and tell them, 'The God of your ancestors has sent me to you,' they won't believe me. They will ask, 'Which god are you talking about? What is his name?'" (Exodus 3:13, NLT)
3. "Moses protested again, 'Look, they won't believe me!'" (Exodus 4:1, NLT)
4. "Moses pleaded with the Lord, 'O Lord, I'm just not a good speaker. I never have been, and I'm not now, even after you have spoken to me. I'm clumsy with words.'" (Exodus 4:10, NLT)
5. "Lord, please! Send someone else." (Exodus 4:13, NLT)

Five times Moses told God he wasn't good enough. Finally, "the Lord became angry with Moses" (Exodus 4:14, NLT). I think

Moses' doubts must have saddened God. He knew that if Moses partnered with him, God would do mighty miracles. God knew Moses was the right person for the job and believed in him, but Moses didn't believe God. Moses was too focused on himself and his limited abilities.

Yet look what was said centuries later about this person who claimed to be clumsy with words. "Moses was taught all the wisdom of the Egyptians, and he became mighty in both speech and action" (Acts 7:22, NLT). God not only worked through Moses, he changed him.

We get so focused on our own self that we become self-conscious instead of God-conscious. How wonderful that God loves us more than we could ever love ourselves. Remember, too, that God uses and works through ordinary people. Whether we know it or not, we are of great worth to our heavenly Father.

Sin

Harboring a sin, a harmful habit, or a bad attitude can block us from hearing God. Sin muffles his voice! When we hear the Lord convicting us but refuse to surrender to his lordship, we continue in sin. Proverbs 1:23 says, "If you had responded to my rebuke, I would have poured out my heart to you and made my thoughts known to you."

If we want the Lord to speak to us, then we must respond to what God has revealed to us about our sin. How wonderful, though, that the Lord provides a way for this barrier to come down—confession and repentance on our part. If we choose not to conceal our sin, then God promises us mercy. "He who conceals his sins does not prosper, but whoever confesses and renounces them finds mercy" (Proverbs 28:13).

Anger toward God

Some people do not want to listen to God because they are angry with him. Possibly they believe God has not treated them

or their loved ones fairly. God understands those kinds of feelings, and he is big enough to handle them. When I am upset or
angry with God, however, I need to be reminded that he has
never done anything wrong! He will help us as we admit our
anger, and in its place he will give us peace. Do not let anger
rob you of an intimate relationship with Jesus Christ.

CAN YOU "FAIL" WHEN YOU FOLLOW PROMPTINGS?

Sometimes we may think God has prompted us to do something, only to find when we follow that leading that the
outcome isn't what we had expected.

That has happened to me. Sometimes I have sensed the
Lord leading me to pray fervently for someone. At times I have
then felt led to call and tell that person that I have been praying.
More than once someone has thanked me for my prayers but
can't identify any specific need. It's a bit humbling! However,
if my prayers and follow-up edify or encourage that person
in some way, then that kindness is a fruit of the Spirit. If you
follow an inner prompting that is in line with what Jesus would
do for that person, then as our daughter Mandy says, "What do
you have to lose?"

I learned this lesson from a young girl I'll call Carrie, who
lived in my former neighborhood. I knew Carrie had a rough
life. She lived with her mother who, along with her live-in
boyfriends, was into partying. Many times Carrie was purposely
locked out of her house. She would then randomly choose a
neighbor and ask if she could come inside. Often she would ask
for food, so several neighbors provided light lunches for her.

My heart went out to this child. Yet it was hard to know
how to reach out to her because she had been hardened at
such a tender age. If the neighbors did not keep their garage
doors closed when she was around, belongings would mysteriously disappear. From the time she was four, she was
permitted to ride her bike up and down the streets of our

subdivision. Since there were no sidewalks, drivers had to watch out for her.

I got to know her a little better when she started school because I worked at the school playground. She alienated everyone. Often I had to break up a fight that she had started during noon recess. Many times she would tell me, her eyes brimming with tears, that she didn't have any friends.

One winter day when she was in fourth grade, I noticed that she did not have any boots. Her feet were always wet and cold. I was pretty sure that the Lord had put it on my heart to purchase a pair of snow boots for her. I had received a thirty-five-dollar check for Christmas from a friend. It didn't seem right that I had so much and Carrie didn't even have a pair of boots.

After checking to make sure it was okay with her mom, I asked Carrie, "Would you like to go to the store with me to get a pair of boots?"

A big smile crossed her face as she said yes. I decided to take two of my daughters with me. Before we picked Carrie up, I told my girls that after we bought her a pair of boots we would all go out for ice cream. We were in a grand mood.

I picked Carrie up at her house. The moment she got into our van she looked at my children and said, "Why did you come?" Next she began demanding to go to McDonald's. She grumbled and complained all the way to the shoe store.

I had decided to take her to a shoe store downtown. I thought it would be fun for her to sit down and be waited on. When we parked the van and she realized where we were going she seemed pleased. I thought, *Oh, good, she will really appreciate this experience.* My good thoughts did not last long. The moment she got into the store it was sheer chaos! She ran all over the store, leaping over small leather stools and jumping onto the chairs. I was embarrassed and my children were humiliated. Other customers gave me looks that clearly asked, "Why can't you do something with *your* child?" I wanted to shout at the top of my lungs, "She is not *my* child!"

Max, the store owner, patiently brought out one pair of boots after another for Carrie to try on. Clearly she was milking this for all it was worth. "I don't like those!" she exclaimed loudly. "Do I have to have *those* boots?" she whined. At last she found the perfect pair and we were all relieved.

As I went to pay for the boots, Carrie ran over to the store's bubble gum machine and demanded that I give her money for a piece. When I wouldn't, she turned to my two children and shouted, "You two kids have to sit in the backseat of the van. I'm sitting in the front." Mandy and Abby looked at me. We exchanged glances that said, "Let her have her way."

For since the world began, no ear has heard, and no eye has seen a God like you, who works for those who wait for him!

Isaiah 64:4, NLT

We were so exhausted by her rude behavior and loud demands that I decided not to take her to get ice cream. Fortunately I had not told her ahead of time about my original plans.

Carrie climbed into the front seat. "I don't want to go home!" she wailed. "I want to do something else like go out for ice cream." She complained all the way home and didn't bother to thank me for the boots as she got out. My children and I sat in her driveway for a minute. We were silent, totally worn out from her behavior.

"Mandy and Abby, let's go get some ice cream," I calmly remarked. As we drove to the restaurant, the kids and I reflected on the evening. It was a great teaching time for all of us.

The next day I was on the playground. To my horror, Carrie had taken off her new boots and was walking around in her white boot liners through melted snow puddles and mud!

"Carrie," I called, "please, honey, put your boots back on.

Your liners are going to get all wet and dirty." Reluctantly she put them back on. The following day Carrie was back to wearing her tennis shoes in the snow.

"Carrie, where are your boots?"

"I don't know," she answered vaguely, and ran off. I saw the boots a couple of times the next week but after that I never saw them again.

A few nights later I was reflecting on that listening experience with the Lord while I was washing our dinner dishes. *Father, I guess I didn't hear you right. I probably was not supposed to buy those boots. I think I just got caught up in trying to meet a need.*

Tears slipped down my cheeks and fell into the sink of dirty dishes. I continued, *I was willing to give up my Christmas check for her. It's obvious she has so many needs! This was one small way I could help and it backfired. Father, she got the liners all muddy and laughed about it. Now she doesn't know where her boots are. She doesn't care. And, Lord, she didn't even say thank you.*

A short time later I sat down at my kitchen desk because I heard the Lord whisper some impressions to my heart. This is what I wrote:

Marilyn, I too saw people with needs many centuries ago. They needed something more than boots. I wanted to help because I love them and care so much about them. Just like you wanted to share your thirty-five dollars, I wanted to give too. My gift, though, was worth more than thirty-five dollars. You cannot attach a monetary amount to my gift. That did not matter, however, because I wanted so badly to give to these people in need.

I sent my Son as the Gift, because you see, Marilyn, people need my Gift. They need Jesus! But, sadly there were not many thank yous when I sent my Gift. And you should see the way people drag my Son in the mud today. He, too—my costly Gift— has been set aside. You know how much you wanted Carrie to like your gift because it would help her? You can't know how much I desire people to want and have my gift of Jesus!

Even if I was not supposed to buy Carrie boots, what did I lose? Nothing! In fact, I gained a fresh understanding of the true meaning of Christmas. Maybe this exercise in listening was not so much meant for Carrie as it was for me.

You don't "fail" if your attempts at obedience don't bring the results you expect. Don't give up listening when this occurs. Neither do you miss the mark if you don't hear anything when you still yourself to listen for God's voice. The only real failure comes from giving up on listening or never trying to listen at all.

CHAPTER 13

Reaping the Rewards
of Listening

*N*ot long ago I spoke at a women's luncheon in Michigan. Following my talk, a number of women lined up to speak with me. An elderly woman stood at the end of the line, patiently waiting.

When she finally reached me, she told me her name was Kay. As we chatted, she mentioned that she had lived in California. Since I had grown up there, I asked the name of her hometown.

"Oh, you've probably never heard of it," she said. "It's Canoga Park."

"Oh yes, I have," I said. "I grew up in Reseda right next to Canoga Park. In fact, my mother taught a Bible study at a church in Canoga Park in the 1960s."

Her eyes widened. "What was your mother's name?" she asked.

"Marion Miller," I said.

Kay's face lit up. "She was my Bible teacher! She came every

Wednesday to teach the women at the church where my husband pastored. She was a wonderful Bible teacher, and we all loved her." She shared some other memories she had of my mother, which I have since passed on to my own children. Kay said my mother was "an incredible woman of God, and everybody loved her."

I was amazed to meet someone who knew and remembered my mother nearly forty years after her death. Perhaps more striking was that I had not mentioned that I was from California or anything about my parents during my talk. In fact, I don't even remember why Kay mentioned where she was from. What was the chance of our not only being in the same room but actually discovering the connection we had through my mother?

When I told her how thankful I was that she had stayed to talk with me, she said, "Well, actually I wasn't planning to because I have to drive a friend home. However, I felt so strongly nudged by the Lord to stay and talk with you that I couldn't leave."

She smiled and said, "I guess you could call that listening to God."

I guess you could. Because Kay followed the Spirit's gentle nudging, we were both encouraged—and since I had been thinking so much about my mother while writing this book, I was pleased that Kay could confirm much of what I remembered about her.

BENEFITS OF LISTENING TO GOD

God works in amazing ways through those who stop to listen to his voice. I have learned that listening is crucial in my spiritual growth, my family life, my other relationships, and my ministry. I cannot function without the Lord's input each day.

Here are just a few of the benefits I've discovered:

Listening to God makes you more Christlike

My friend Barb Cline once encouraged me to spend time asking the Lord to give me a word or a phrase that he would like to work on with me throughout the year. I call this exercise in listening "a word for the year." Every September I ask the Lord for the word or phrase that he would like me to work on the following year. Several ideas usually pop into my head right away. However, after I take time to wait on him, he always clarifies the word or phrase he desires. By January 1, I have a new word for the year, and it is always specifically for me. (In the past, I had made New Year's resolutions but always forgot about them as the months passed. Concentrating on the one word that God impressed on my heart was more manageable; it stuck with me.)

A couple of years ago my word for the year was *adjust*. The Lord seemed to be asking me to be willing to adjust to whatever he allowed in my life. At times I needed to adjust an attitude; in other situations I needed to be more flexible. The year was filled with physical pain and everyday inconveniences. The question became: How quickly could I adjust to his plans in any given situation?

One morning as I walked through our dining room, I stepped on wet carpet. *How did this happen?* I wondered, since our house was new. I decided to check the garage, which was next to the dining room. The garage wall was wet and there was a puddle of water on the floor. *A pipe must have broken,* I concluded. I then checked our basement. Water was running down the cement block walls of the storage room directly under the dining room. Cardboard boxes were soaked. I groaned.

I called the plumber, who eventually tore into the garage wall to see what was causing the leak. He called me a little later and said, "You'd better call your insurance company!" The installers who put up shelving in our garage had hammered the nails right into the main sewer pipe that led from the upstairs toilet. Ugh! So that was the source of the "water" in the dining room, garage, and basement. The plumber suggested that the shelf installer may not have used a stud finder before pounding in the nails.

I went back into the house, upset that such a silly mistake could have caused so many problems. As I was getting ready to dial our insurance agent, the old familiar prompting came to my heart. *Marilyn, can you adjust to me in this situation too? Watch your words and attitude as you speak with the agent.* I took a deep breath.

I finally reached the person I needed to talk with. After explaining the situation and talking through the insurance options, the agent said she couldn't believe how calm I was. I laughed and said, "Well, I can either cry and be upset about this or laugh and see what good will come out of the situation."

She then said, "I see that your last name is Hontz. Are you by any chance Marilyn Hontz, the speaker who talks about prayer? I heard you speak . . ." I don't remember the rest of the conversation except how grateful I was to the Lord who had helped me keep my cool.

The best part of this whole ordeal, however, was that I had an opportunity to share Christ with our insurance agent. She had received Christ as a child but had not walked with him. She ended up recommitting her life to Christ, which in turn affected her husband and daughter. Together they became involved in a church as a family for the first time.

My experience with our sewer pipe eventually was used for good. The carpets and walls cleaned up, a family found Jesus, and I learned that the Lord can always bring good out of frustrating situations if I will adjust to him.

Whether you are just learning to listen to God or are a seasoned listener, ask him to give you a word or phrase that he would like to work on in your life. Other words I have concentrated on in the past are *hospitality, prayer, listening, encourager,* and *abide.*

Whenever I speak to groups, I always encourage those who want to begin listening for God's voice to try this exercise. Finding a "word for the year" is really a meaningful listening adventure with the Lord. By the time the Holy Spirit and I have worked together on a word for twelve months, I can usually see some growth in that area. That encourages me to want to grow more.

Listening to God leads to a greater awareness and a deeper understanding of him

For the last two years, I have been asking the Lord to help me think about him more during my day. I was inspired by some of the writings of Frank Laubauch, who was a pioneer in literacy and a missionary to the Philippines. I was challenged by his desire to try to think about God as much as possible during the day. I put that idea together with some thoughts from Brother Lawrence, author of *Practicing the Presence,* and A. W. Tozer, who wrote about having a "preoccupation with God." That was what I wanted—to be preoccupied with Jesus and to think about him *more* each day.

While I am far from achieving this lofty goal, the Holy Spirit is faithful in helping me turn my thoughts toward God when I ask for his assistance. I often go hours at a time with no thoughts of the Lord, then I suddenly have a fresh awareness of his presence and he floods my thoughts. I love when that happens. I call those my "God moments."

In time, I told the Lord that I would also like to think about him in the middle of night if I happened to wake up. I decided to picture the Lord Jesus at the right side of my bed. Whenever I go to sleep each night, I envision him sitting there. Then, as soon as I wake up in the morning, I remember that he is right there and that he is going to go through my day with me.

The Lord took me up on my desire to be awakened during the night. Perhaps our thoughts are quieter and our mind is more "unedited" during those hours. Usually sometime between 2:30 and 5:30 A.M., I wake up for just a few seconds and simply tell the Lord that I love him. I then go right back to sleep.

This past June, I awoke and my thoughts instantly turned to the Lord. I whispered, "I love you, Jesus." Suddenly, I was aware of the presence of God in a very powerful way. It was as if he was standing right at my bedside. His presence was so awesome and overwhelming that I began to silently weep, so as not to disturb my sleeping husband. I had caught a small glimpse of his holiness, his majesty, and his righteousness.

Even as I sensed his holiness, I saw who I was. A sinner! The contrast was huge—bigger than huge! At that moment there were no buddy-buddy feelings in my heart toward God. Instead the passage from Isaiah 6 came to my mind. *Lord,* I said silently, *I feel like the prophet Isaiah who said, "Woe to me." I, too, am a person of "unclean lips."* Tears continued to trickle down my face as I poured out my heart to the Lord and confessed that I was, indeed, a sinner.

Then the gentle voice of the Lord called to me from the depths of my heart, *Yes, my child, you are a sinner, but you have been washed in the blood of Jesus Christ. When I look at you I see a white robe of righteousness covering you.*

But, Lord, I continued, *I don't feel like I deserve to be near you.*

Marilyn, look. I am approachable.

In spite of the incredible difference between me and the Lord, he was reassuring me that I *could* draw near to him. He was and is approachable, and he welcomes me and *all* his children who desire to be close to him.

I am still being profoundly impacted by that experience. I realize that only when we behold him one day in heaven will we truly experience the presence of God in all his fullness. I also realize that while it is impossible for me to dwell on him all day long now, it *will* be possible in heaven. I want to practice turning my thoughts toward him now! I want to hear his voice in the middle of the day or night. I believe our yearning and hungering for God brings him great delight. To think that our listening to God can bring him delight is incredible. What a huge benefit!

Listening to God helps you in your family life

One evening as I was getting ready for bed, I heard the still, small voice of the Holy Spirit. He prompted me to ask our daughter Holly how she was doing. She was in high school and was up late studying.

That's kind of strange, Father, I remember thinking. *I just said good night to her, and if I ask her how she is doing, I'm sure she will tell me that everything is fine.*

I then heard the Lord say it again. *Ask her how she is doing, and mention this name.* I had no idea why I was to mention that person's name.

I went down the hall and asked Holly how she was doing.

"Fine, Mom," she said with a smile.

"No, really, Holly, how are you?" I continued.

"Mom, really, I am fine."

Finally I said, "Are you okay about _____?" I mentioned the person's name that I sensed the Lord had given me. Instantly, she began crying. The tears turned to sobbing. I had no idea what a floodgate I had just opened.

She was crying so hard that my husband heard her and came upstairs. He peeked his head into the room long enough to know that he needed to pray for Holly. He sat in the hallway outside her door and prayed the entire time I was in Holly's bedroom.

Hurt upon hurt came out of Holly. Everything seemed to tumble out, beginning with hurts inflicted in the third grade by some girlfriends when she went over to play. With sadness

I remembered watching as her two friends had pointed and laughed at her. They whispered to each other and then ran away, leaving Holly alone on the sidewalk. The rejection of that event was deeply ingrained in Holly's memory.

Memory after memory of hurtful relationships flushed their way out. Holly needed healing. I had no idea that she was carrying those damaging memories so carefully inside—but the Lord did. The Lord says that he is "close to the brokenhearted and saves those who are crushed in spirit" (Psalm 34:18). That night, with much prayer, God freed Holly from the memories that had held her captive. She was released to be the person God had made her to be. That night was a turning point for her.

How wonderful that the Lord allowed her mom and dad to come alongside her to help in that journey to wholeness. How wonderful that Holly was able to work through that "baggage" early in life. I am so thankful the Holy Spirit alerted me to the invisible needs of one of my own children. There are huge benefits to listening to God as you parent!

Listening to God enriches your friendships

I am amazed at how listening to the Lord affects all aspects of our life, including our relationships. My dear friend Jimmy Johnson used to say, "If we would ever learn to give birth to our impulses of love, perhaps we would discover for the first time what it means to be led by the Holy Spirit." Listening to God helps us to "give birth" to those impulses of love that we feel nudged to act on.

One morning while I was reading the Word and meditating on a verse, the Lord impressed upon me to send that verse to a friend to encourage her. I wrote it out and mailed it to her. I knew she and her husband were traveling in Europe, and I hoped that the verse would brighten her day when she returned home to some heavy responsibilities.

Some weeks later I got a letter back from my friend. She

said that while she was in Europe, the Lord had showed her a verse from Scripture that she was literally clinging to. She showed the verse to her husband, and together they claimed it as a promise from the Lord for their situation. When she returned home she opened my letter. The verse I included in my letter was the same one the Holy Spirit had shown her! We were both so blessed by what the Lord had done. When you sense that the Lord Jesus wants you to do something, do it!

> *I listen carefully to what God the Lord is saying.*
> **Psalm 85:8, NLT**

Recently I almost missed out on an opportunity to encourage someone because I didn't obey a prompting as soon as I should have. During my morning prayer time I clearly heard the Lord tell me to call a woman named Sandy from our church. She had been battling cancer. I knew the prompting was to call her that *morning*. I wrote her name on a piece of paper and placed it on the kitchen counter. I looked at that slip throughout the morning but told myself, *I'll call her later*. That afternoon I ran into Sandy and her husband at the grocery store. She had just returned from the doctor's office.

"Marilyn, I got difficult news this morning," she said. "The doctor told me that I have months, not the years I thought I had, to live." Her husband wrapped his arms around her shoulders as she struggled to give me the news. "I only have months," she repeated softly.

My heart was breaking. I wished so much that I had called her when I was first prompted. I had no idea she was going to the doctor that day, but God knew. She might have been encouraged to come home from the doctor's office to find a message on her answering machine telling her that God had put her name on my heart and that I was praying for her. God graciously gave me a second chance to encourage her, but my support might have meant even more had I responded when first prompted.

I love what Mary, Jesus' mother, said when she and Jesus were at a wedding in Cana. The wine ran out, and Mary went to Jesus with the problem. She then told the servants, "Do whatever he tells you" (John 2:5). What a powerful phrase. I long to be found doing whatever Jesus tells me to do!

Listening to God helps you in everyday situations

Listening to the Lord has helped me many times when I have been working. One bitterly cold day I was helping out on the playground during noon recess. I was wearing snow pants, a jacket, boots, a scarf, and two pairs of mittens, but I was still cold! As I looked around, I spotted an eight-year-old girl who was not dressed properly. Her spring coat with its broken zipper and her tennis shoes were no match for this weather. I watched her come toward me, shivering as she walked.

"Mrs. Hontz," she said softly, "I'm cold."

"I'm sure you are, Becca," I responded gently. "Go on up by the building, and I will see about borrowing a coat for you to wear out here today."

I knew the office had spare coats, but I also knew I needed to buy her a new one. I checked in the office and asked if they thought Becca's mom would mind if I purchased a new coat for her. The secretary replied that the mom would probably be very grateful, and I received an okay.

I went home after the recess break, called my husband, and told him about Becca. "Go out and get her a coat right away," he said. I knew JCPenney was offering 25 percent off all jackets. *I'll go there,* I decided.

However, as I put my hand on the doorknob to go to the store, I again felt that whispering in my heart. *Marilyn, you didn't pray about this.*

Oh, Father, I replied, *this is something I know you would want me to do. I didn't think I had to pray about it.*

The prompting continued. I knew I needed to make time to

pray and listen to the Lord before I went to the store. I put down my car keys and knelt down by our blue sofa. *Okay, Lord, I'm listening, what am I supposed to do?*

As I listened and waited, the Holy Spirit put on my heart the name of a different store—the Outpost. It did not make sense to me at all.

That's a great store, Father; however, it seems to me that they never have any sales. They are out of my budget, I argued.

The guidance remained the same: *Call Outpost; I want the best for Becca.*

Finally, I got up the courage and dialed the store. I reached the manager and stammered a bit, asking if they had any children's coats on sale. She replied that they didn't.

I said quietly to the Lord, *See, Lord, I told you they don't have sales there.*

Next I asked if they had some coats from last year—last year's models—in their back room. Again the reply was no.

Sensing I was uncomfortable, the manager asked what specifically I was looking for. I explained that my husband and I wanted to purchase a size 10 jacket for a little girl at a local school.

"Oh, it's interesting that you called," the manager said eagerly. "I just received a call from the police station. Every year they submit the name of a child who needs a coat. This year they did not have a name. Tell us about the little girl."

I explained that she did not have a winter coat and that her mom could not afford one. My husband and I wanted to help by purchasing one for her. "How soon can you get down to the store?" she asked.

"I can be there in about ten minutes," I replied.

"We will have a coat for her when you come in," she announced.

"Okay, I'll be there in a few minutes to purchase the coat," I replied, wondering at the same time how I was going to pay for it.

"Oh no, you don't understand," the manager interrupted. "You don't have to pay for it. We want to do this." I couldn't believe my ears.

I drove to the store and walked up to the counter. A huge bag sat there. I inquired about the coat for the little girl, and they pointed to the bag. The clerk began to pull items out of the bag: a Columbia brand jacket, snow pants, mittens, and a hat . . . it was incredible! As the clerk was handing me the bag, she added a pair of heavy socks. I was in shock. I just thought I was going to pick up a jacket, and now I had a whole snow outfit.

I drove back home thanking the Lord all the way. I called the school secretary and told her I had a coat and other clothes for Becca. I asked if I could drop it off in the office.

When I got to the school, both the secretary and principal were waiting for me. After I showed them all the clothes, they were in tears. The secretary called Becca into the office and showed her the big bag of clothes. Her face was radiant. She wanted to try everything on! As the secretary was helping to pull off her socks, we couldn't help but notice that the socks she had on were full of holes. I really didn't know how they stayed on her feet. I had no idea her socks had holes, but the Lord did. He had put it on that manager's heart to include socks too! Becca went back to class wearing her snowsuit. It was a tender scene.

As I started to leave the office, the secretary thanked me for what I had done. "No, you don't understand. I didn't do anything; it was God who got Becca the clothes." I then explained what had happened. The secretary asked me if we could get together for lunch sometime. We made a date for her to come over to my home for lunch. A few days later, sitting at my kitchen table, the secretary said that when she was a little girl she had received the Lord, but she wanted to recommit her life to Christ.

Shortly after that incident, I came across this verse in my Bible: "Whether you turn to the right or to the left, your ears will hear a voice behind you, saying, 'This is the way; walk in it'"

(Isaiah 30:21). Such personalized guidance is what God wanted to give me as I was on my way out the door to go to JCPenney. Praise the Lord that we have a God who wants to speak to us and guide us!

That incident showed me how important it is to check with the Lord on everything. Even if something sounds good, he may (and usually does) have a better plan. A. W. Tozer said, "God is looking for people through whom He can do the impossible—what a pity that we plan only the things we can do by ourselves."[23]

My plan was to go to JCPenney. God's plan was the impossible. He wanted the best for Becca. He knew that if I went to JCPenney I could only afford a jacket, and she needed a lot more than that.

I also saw that God wants to use his children to accomplish *his* purposes. He can do anything with just a word, but he chooses to let us partner with him! He is actually asking us to be an extension of Jesus!

So many of my prayers used to be, *Please, Father, would you give me this and would you do that?* While it's fine to ask—in fact we are encouraged to ask, seek, and knock (Matthew 7:7)—I now want to be sure I ask what he would like from me. My daily prayer needs to be, *Lord, how do you want to use me today, and how can I partner with you?* There is a definite shift as we go from making God our errand boy to becoming *his* errand person.

I've heard that each morning when he gets up, pastor Jack Hayford kneels by his bed and says, "I am a servant of the Most High God." What a great way to get focused and put things in true perspective.

Listening to God enables you to minister to others

Just before Easter this year, during one of my listening prayer times, the Lord very clearly reminded me how much Jesus had done for me by dying on the cross. He had forgiven my sins, and he was preparing a place for me in heaven. I began to focus on the Cross and the pain that Jesus chose to endure for me. The Lord impressed upon me that I needed to share more with others about what Jesus has done for me.

I began to weep as it hit me in a fresh way how this "Man of sorrows," who was "acquainted with grief," had paid a huge price not only for me, but for everyone (Isaiah 53:3, NKJV).

I said to the Lord, *It's not fair that I should know you and so many others don't. Father, I sense that you have challenged me in a new way to share your Good News. Please, help me to verbally share my faith with anyone you want to bring into my life.*

It is much easier for me to walk the Christian walk rather than *verbally* share my faith. I reminded him that since I was writing this book, I was "tucked away" and did not have as much contact with people. In fact, sad to say, I could not think of one person in my life who needed Jesus. I also did not have one unsaved person's name down on my prayer list! I ended my listening time by saying, *Father, I want to be obedient and attentive to you. With your help, I am available to share about you. Even though I do not think of myself as a soul winner and it's a bit scary at times, I will verbally share my faith. Would you please bring an unsaved person to me?* (Watch out! God loves to answer that type of prayer!)

A few days later I received a call from our church office. A woman named Jeanie who lived in a distant city had called and asked to talk to me. She told Anna, a ministry assistant, that she had heard me on a *Focus on the Family* radio broadcast.

Anna suggested that the woman leave her phone number and promised to pass the message on to me. Anna didn't know the reason Jeanie wanted to talk to me.

I was very busy when Anna gave me the message. I had houseguests, and lots of cooking to do, plus I was trying to write. To be honest, I put the call off for a couple of days. The Lord, however, kept prompting me to return Jeanie's phone call.

Finally, I called her. She was so grateful that I had returned her call, and she told me that she had heard my story on the radio three years before. She asked me, "Are you trained to help people?"

Thinking that she was asking if I was a professional counselor, I said, "No, but I can listen, and perhaps recommend some materials for you or suggest a counselor."

Jeanie graciously replied, "Well, I don't need a counselor. I need a trained person who can tell me about God. Can you do that?"

I almost started laughing with joy. "Yes," I replied, "I can tell you about God."

> *I stand at the door and knock. If anyone hears my voice and opens the door, I will come in and eat with him, and he with me.*
>
> **Jesus, in Revelation 3:20**

At that exact moment the Holy Spirit whispered to my heart, *I am sending someone into your life to share with—are you available?*

I replied, *Yes, Lord, if you will help me, I will be obedient.*

Jeanie told me that she came from a very religious background but wanted to know God better. I asked, "Have you ever invited Jesus Christ to come into your life as your Savior, Lord, and Friend?"

She said, "No, but *that's* what I want to do!"

Again, because she said she was religious, I asked her, "Has anyone ever taken the time to share with you from the Bible what it means to be born again?"

Again, she said no. I asked if it would be okay if I shared some Scriptures with her. She said yes and my heart began pounding wildly.

I started with the Gospel of John chapter 3, and showed her how a religious man by the name of Nicodemus came to Jesus with the same question she had. Jesus explained to him that it wasn't enough just to be "religious." He told Nicodemus (two times, in fact) that he *must* be "born again." It was imperative! This being born again thing was not a church or denomination's idea—it was Jesus' idea.

Jeanie listened silently as I took her through nine more verses from the Bible that explained how she could have a personal, dynamic relationship with Jesus Christ. One of those verses I turned to was Romans 3:23. I explained that *all* of us have sinned, and that we have *all* fallen short of God's standard. I shared an illustration at this point.

"Suppose three of us were standing on the Pacific beach in California. We all decided that we wanted to swim to Hawaii. Let's say that I started out first and got five miles out into the ocean before I had to stop. You then tried and got ten miles out to sea before you stopped. Then an Olympic swimmer tried and he was able to swim one hundred miles before he finally had to quit. Now, who made it to Hawaii?" I asked.

"No one," she answered.

I replied, "That's exactly my point. All three had good intentions but no one reached the goal; they all fell short. So we, too, because of our sin, have fallen short of God's standards.

"But, Jeanie," I quickly reassured her, "God has provided a way for us to have a relationship with him. He has given us the gift of his Son."

After going through a few more verses, she asked, "Do you mean to tell me that all I have to do is ask Jesus to come into my life?"

"Yes," I replied. A few minutes later, Jeanie prayed to ask the Lord to forgive her of her sins and invited him to be Savior and Lord of her life.

She became a new creation in Christ! She has begun a journey of listening that will last through eternity. My husband sent her materials for her to grow in her new relationship with God, and a couple from our church are discipling her through a correspondence Bible study. We were also able to give her some names of churches in her area. She is so hungry for God.

I'll never forget Jeanie's words after she accepted Christ: "I have wanted this all of my life!"

I could have missed the most important opportunity in the world—to share Jesus. I wonder what would have happened if I had not taken the time to listen to the Lord that morning. I believe if Jeanie had called me before I had been challenged by the Lord to verbally share my faith, I would have allowed fear to stop me. I may have been tempted to say, "My husband is a minister—let me have him call you back and tell you how to know Jesus." I would have missed a great blessing.

You know, sharing your faith is simply telling *your* story in the power of the Holy Spirit and leaving the results to him. All the Father asks is that we be available. He does all the rest.

MAKING THE JOURNEY YOUR OWN

My mother left me a listening legacy—what legacy will *you* leave for future generations? Will you accept the challenge and embark on a journey of recognizing God's voice through Scripture, prayer, and listening? Any sacrifices you make cannot compare with the rewards you will reap. Any challenges you face will be worthwhile in light of the spiritual heritage you will leave for those who come behind you. So don't wait. Accept the command spoken to the Israelites: "Listen to his voice, and cling to him" (Deuteronomy 13:4, NLT).

First, *expect* God to speak! If you doubt he will speak to you, ask him for increased faith. My husband told me the other day, "I believe God is speaking all the time but we're not usually listening. The reason you hear him, Marilyn, is because you expect him to speak to you." I had not considered that before, but I realized that he was right: I do expect God to speak. Just as I know my husband will answer me when I ask him a question, I expect the Lord to answer me. I like what author John Eldredge says about this: "I don't think [God] speaks to me any more than others; I think I've just learned to expect it, need it, keep an eye out for it. It's a whole different perspective on how we approach our day."[24]

Second, strive to grow in your desire to be *attentive* to the Holy Spirit. I know it is easy to be distracted, but God has power over all of our restless, wandering thoughts! Ask him to help you be more attentive to him throughout your day. Stopping to listen for God's voice does not come naturally at first—or all the time—for anyone.

Third, invite God to *interrupt* you. If your heavenly Father wanted to, could he interrupt you at any time during your day to ask you to do something *with* him? I used to view interruptions in life as a nuisance and a hindrance. Now I see them as opportunities. Frank Laubauch suggested asking God: "What are you doing in the world today that I can help you with?"[25] Ask the Lord to free you up to be ready whenever he needs you. He is continually teaching me to be more flexible and spontaneous, two qualities I do not come by naturally.

After the Holy Spirit has your attention, then be *available.* Are you available to follow his promptings? It could be to get a coat for a needy child, send an encouraging note to someone, or share your faith. . . . who knows what God wants to do through you!

Finally, listening all comes down to this: *obedience.* You may expect God to speak, you may be attentive, interruptible, and available throughout your day, but it is only through obedience that you can be an extension of Jesus Christ in your world.

Each morning I seek to say to the Lord: *Father, today I expect you to speak; now help me to be attentive, interruptible, available, and obedient to your Holy Spirit. Let me hear what you want to say, and don't let me miss what you want me to accomplish today with your help.* He waits for a similar invitation from you.

Learn to listen for God. If you do, you are in for an incredible journey, and you will soon have your own stories of divine appointments to tell. Because, you see, listening is for life—both here on earth and in eternity.

> Lord, teach me to listen. The times are noisy and my ears are weary with the thousand raucous sounds which continuously assault them. Give me the spirit of the boy Samuel when he said to Thee, 'Speak, for thy servant heareth.' Let me hear Thee speaking in my heart. Let me get used to the sound of Thy voice, that its tones may be familiar when the sounds of earth die away and the only sound will be the music of Thy speaking voice. Amen.[26]

QUESTIONS TO THINK ABOUT:

1. Have you ever been prompted by the Holy Spirit to do something for someone else? Did you follow the prompting? What were the results?

2. According to chapter 11, "Listening to God is not seeking 'inside information.'" What does that mean, and what kind of insights *does* God give us when we listen to him?

3. Have you ever asked God to help you plan your daily to-do list? If so, what was your experience? If not, how could you incorporate this into your listening time?

4. What are some ways you can better deal with distractions during your quiet times with God?

5. How does busyness interfere with your ability to hear God speak? What can you do about it?

6. The Holy Spirit not only desires to speak during our quiet times, but *throughout* our day. How can you become more aware of his voice or more "preoccupied with him" during your busy day?

7. What benefit of listening to God appeals to you most?

8. What does Psalm 46:10 mean to you? ("Be still, and know that I am God; I will be exalted among the nations, I will be exalted in the earth.")

9. Will you commit yourself to asking the Lord each day how he would like to use you to share his love with others? How do you think your life would be affected by such a request?

Bible Study Tools

Step into the Bible section of any bookstore and you are likely to be overwhelmed by the wide variety of Bibles and study tools available. If Bible study is new to you—or you just want a reminder of what is available—the following information will help orient you to the tools you can use as you study Scripture.*

Bible Versions

In general, Bible translators approach their task with either a "word for word" or a "thought for thought" approach. A "word for word" translator attempts to translate each word of the original language as precisely as possible—and to follow the original word order and sentence structure as much as possible too. These translations are particularly valuable for those who

---

*If reading the Bible is new to you, *No-Brainer's Guide to the Bible* (Wheaton, Ill.: Tyndale House, 2001) by James S. Bell Jr. and James Dyet may be helpful. It contains an overview of each book of the Bible, along with a one-year Bible reading program and other helpful features.

have some familiarity with Scripture and want to study passages at a more scholarly level.

The goal of the "thought for thought" translator is to produce the closest natural equivalent of the message expressed in the original text—both in meaning and style. The goal is to be accurate *and* readable. These translations are particularly valuable to those who are new to the Bible and want the clearest wording possible.

Word for Word ▲ New American Standard Bible
King James Version
New King James Version
New Revised Standard Version
New International Version
New Living Translation
Contemporary English Version
Thought for Thought ▼ The Living Bible

Other Study Tools

Bible Atlas—Many Bibles include a few maps at the back, but if you're a visual learner you may appreciate having a complete book of maps so you can locate places mentioned in Scripture.

Concordance—This tool provides an alphabetical listing of words mentioned in the Bible, along with the Scripture references where each is found. It is a handy tool to help you locate a verse when all you remember is a word or phrase from it. Again, many Bibles contain an abbreviated version; however, you may wish to invest in a complete concordance.

Commentaries—As the name implies, these tools include comments from Bible scholars on a book of the Bible. They can help provide the context and background that makes reading Scripture come alive! Shop carefully for these, since some are geared toward scholars while others are written with the novice in mind.

Bible Dictionary—Like a regular dictionary, a Bible dictionary lists topics alphabetically. It provides correct spellings and—more important—additional information on various biblical topics.

A Prayer Test

*W*hat kind of pray-er are you?*

1. *Crisis Pray-er*—You pray only when there is a problem.
2. *Casual Pray-er*—You pray when you have the time or when you remember. You don't set aside a regular time to pray.
3. *Committed Pray-er*—You have a set, daily time of prayer. You pray for those for whom you've promised you would.
4. *Intercessor*—You pray daily. You continue to pray for the needs of others long after others have stopped praying about those needs. Prayer is foremost on your heart; it is your passion.

*Dr. Alvin J. VanderGriend, national facilitator of Lighthouse Ministries for the Mission America Coalition, challenged me with this prayer test. Used with permission.

T.A.W.G.
(Time Alone with God)

*L*istening for God's voice in the everyday moments of life will bring you greater joy and purpose. That is why I have made this the focus of *Listening for God*. However, I have also discovered great value in devoting several hours now and then—even an occasional day—to inviting God to speak to my heart.

The acronym T.A.W.G. (Time Alone with God) is commonly recognized within the denomination in which my husband and I minister. Our church's pastors and staff members are encouraged to take a D.A.W.G. (Day Alone with God) once a month to refocus on the Lord and his calling on their life. Because I believe the practice will enrich the life of any Christian, I regularly recommend it to others.

T.A.W.G. can take many forms. You might choose to spend an *hour* with God (H.A.W.G.) or an entire *day* with him (D.A.W.G.). Regardless of how much time you set aside to have a T.A.W.G., I suggest that you plan a flexible agenda and find a solitary place.

An agenda will give you direction and keep your mind focused. Perhaps you will decide to read and reflect upon a book of the Bible, such as Ephesians. Or maybe you will come prepared to study all the words on grace in the Bible. You may even plan to take a nap. (Sometimes sleeping is the most spiritual thing you can do.)

Make sure your agenda is flexible enough, however, for the Holy Spirit to break through and adjust your goals. I offer some suggestions to help you plan your own T.A.W.G. day. You may wish to incorporate some of these ideas or plan something else entirely. This is an appointment between you and your Heavenly Father.

What to bring:
- your Bible
- a pen
- a notepad or journal
- a desire to be with God, hear from God, and enjoy God

This time alone with the Lord is not an obligation, but an incredible opportunity. It is never a duty for God to spend time with *you.*

1. Find a place that is free from distractions.

Get alone, and "plan to neglect" other things. Jesus himself had to do the same thing.

> *Very early in the morning, while it was still dark, Jesus got up, left the house and went off to a* solitary *place, where he prayed. Simon and his companions went to look for him, and when they found him, they exclaimed: "Everyone is looking for you!" (Mark 1:35-37, emphasis mine)*

Jesus not only got away to a solitary place, but he also encouraged his disciples to do the same. There will always be people who want you or things that need your attention. Jesus experienced this on earth as well. He knows how much we need these times of restoration.

> *Then, because so many people were coming and going that they did not even have a chance to eat, he said to [the disciples], "Come with me by yourselves to a quiet place and get some rest." So they went away by themselves in a boat to a solitary place. (Mark 6:31-32, emphasis mine)*

2. Once you are at your solitary place, picture Jesus waiting for you.

There is pure joy on his face at the sight of you. The Lord longs for you and treasures you more than you realize. A. W. Tozer said, "He waits to be wanted."

3. Quiet yourself, and then ask for the Lord's presence.

> *Dear Father, I want to be still and close to you. Help me to quiet the noisy places in my life. Help me to let go of all that I am currently preoccupied with and instead to be preoccupied with your Son, Jesus. I now invite you, Holy Spirit, who is full of peace, to rain down on me. Help me to hear your voice only. I pray this in Jesus' name. Amen.*

4. If distractions come to your thoughts (and they will), ask the Lord to help you focus on him.

You may suddenly remember something that you must do. Write it down on your notepad to do later. Remember that Satan is the "master distracter." He does not want you to have time alone with the Lord Jesus. Remember St. Francis of Assisi's words: "If your heart wanders or is distracted, bring it back and replace it tenderly in the presence of the Master. Even if you have to do this all hour—your hour would still be well employed." That is encouraging! Our time with the Lord is never wasted time.

5. Begin with adoration and praise to the Lord.

> *Enter his gates with thanksgiving and his courts with praise. (Psalm 100:4)*

- Take time to adore him.
- Dwell on his names from Scripture: Prince of Peace, Counselor, Great Physician, King of kings, Burden Bearer, and Friend of sinners, to name a few.
- Which of his names do you need him to be for you right now?
- Praise him for who he is.
- Praise him, as well, for the difficult situations in your life right now.
- Praise him that he can be trusted and that he has his children's best interests at heart.

6. Seek to confess any known sin.

> *"Search me, O God, and know my heart . . . see if there is any offensive way in me" (Psalm139:23-24). I realize that sin separates me from you and muffles your voice. Please, Lord, help hold me still so that your Holy Spirit may search me.*

At this point, stop and be quiet before the Lord. Listen.
- Did the Lord reveal anything?
- Are you holding bitterness or resentment toward someone?
- Do you need to forgive one who has wronged you?
- Do you need to ask someone to forgive you?

If nothing comes to mind, thank him for his cleansing power. If the Lord reveals a specific sin:

- Write it down
- Confess your sin (*confess* means "to agree with")
- Repent (turn from that sin)
- Receive God's forgiveness
- With your pen, blot out any sin(s) you wrote on your paper
- On the same paper, write out this verse: "If we confess our sins, he is faithful and just and will forgive us our sins and purify us from *all* unrighteousness." (1 John 1:9, emphasis mine)

Just as you blotted out the sin on your paper, so God blots out your confessed sin with the precious blood of his Son Jesus. "I—yes, I alone—am the one who blots out your sins . . . and will never think of them again" (Isaiah 43:25, NLT). He no longer sees your sin! (Keep in mind, however, that if something comes to your remembrance that you have previously confessed, it is your enemy trying to defeat you.) Nineteenth-century evangelist D. L. Moody once said, "God casts our confessed sins into the depths of the sea, and He has even put up a 'No Fishing' sign over the spot."

Continue praying:

Thank you, Lord, that you graciously point out my sin, provide a way for me to get rid of it, and then remember it no more. "For I will forgive their wickedness and will remember their sins no more" (Jeremiah 31:34). Thank you that when you died on the cross you redeemed us so that we could be in relationship with you. "He does not treat us as our sins deserve or repay us according to our iniquities. . . . As far as the east is from the west, so far has he removed our transgressions from us." (Psalm 103:10, 12).

7. After you have spent time in adoration and confession, thank the Lord for all he has done for you. Think of as many things as you can.

> *Every good and perfect gift is from above, coming down from the Father of the heavenly lights. (James 1:17)*

Try to extend your thanksgiving to include even some difficult things you may be experiencing.

> *Give thanks in all circumstances, for this is God's will for you in Christ Jesus. (1 Thessalonians 5:18)*

8. Read Psalm 46:10.

> *Be still, and know that I am God; I will be exalted among the nations, I will be exalted in the earth.*

Jesus himself is asking you to live out this verse. It is not simply a request; it is a command. Meditate on the entire verse. What does it mean to you?

9. As you sit quietly in God's presence, ask him to bring rest to your soul.

> *Come to me, all you who are weary and burdened, and I will give you rest. (Matthew 11:28)*

He can help you relax as you give him your tension and the stressors of the day. Tell him or write out what is heavy on you.

10. Read a chapter from Proverbs. (You might read the chapter that corresponds to the day of the month. For instance, if it's the fifteenth, read chapter 15.) Next, read a psalm of your choice. As you read, ask the Holy Spirit to speak through those verses.

11. Pray:

> *Father, your Word says "do not fret" (Psalm 37:8), "do not be anxious about anything" (Philippians 4:6). I know, Lord Jesus, that worrying is taking on a responsibility you never intended for me to have. Help me to exchange my worries for your peace. Help me to trust you with these matters. Thank you that your Word says that nothing is too difficult for you. Nothing.*

Read Philippians 4:6-8.
- Ask the Lord to reveal any worries that may be weighing you down.
- List your cares on paper.
- Next to your list, write the verse: "Cast all your anxiety on him because he cares for you" (1 Peter 5:7).
- Now picture the Cross.
- Visualize yourself dropping all those burdens at the foot of the Cross. Leave them there!
- We have a big God! He is *able!* God is *enough!*

12. Turn to Romans 12:9-21. As you read this passage, ask the Lord this question:

> *Father is there a word or phrase you want to whisper to my heart?*

Take time to listen, then ask:

> *Father, is there anything you would like me to do with you that will make a difference for eternity?*

Again, take time to listen.

13. If the Lord brings something to mind, write it down. He may prompt you to pray for someone. (Take time at this point to intercede for others.) The Lord may lead you to write a note or to serve him in a certain way. He may or may not reveal a word at this time. Don't feel discouraged if you did not sense his voice. Listening takes time and practice. Just tell the Lord that you are seeking to listen and be obedient to his promptings.

14. End your time alone with God in prayer.

> *Abba Father, thank you for these quiet moments with you. Help me to learn to stay in loving attentiveness to you. Thank you that you are always attentive to me. I want to think about you more throughout my day. I want to draw closer to you. I desire to be still and know that you are God. Thank You, Father, for leading me beside quiet waters and restoring my soul (Psalm 23:2-3). In Jesus' name I pray, Amen.*

Endnotes

[1] Chuck Smith and Tal Brooke, *Harvest* (Costa Mesa, Calif.: The Word for Today), 141.

[2] Kenneth Kinghorn, ed., *John Wesley on Christian Beliefs: The Standard Sermons in Modern English,* vol. 1, Sermons 1–20 (Nashville: Abingdon Press, 2002), 30.

[3] Oswald Chambers, *If Ye Shall Ask* (Grand Rapids, Mich.: Chosen Books, 1958), 24.

[4] D. M. M'Intyre, *The Hidden Life of Prayer* (Grand Rapids, Mich.: Baker Book House, 1979), 94.

[5] See <http://www.posword.org/articles/gordsd/prayer01.shtml>.

[6] James Houston, *The Transforming Power of Prayer* (Colorado Springs, Colo.: NavPress, 1996), 5.

[7] Joni Eareckson Tada, *Diamonds in the Dust* (Grand Rapids, Mich.: Zondervan, 1993).

[8] Wesley Duewel, *Touch the World through Prayer* (Grand Rapids, Mich.: Francis Asbury Press, 1986), 16.

[9] Corrie ten Boom, *The Hiding Place* (Ulrichsville, Ohio: Barbour Publishing, 1971), 154.

[10] Randy Alcorn, *The Ishband Conspiracy* (Sisters, Ore.: Multnomah Publishers, Inc., 2001), 54.

[11] See <http://www.laymanstraining.com/motivator4.html>.

[12] Richard Foster, *Prayer: Finding the Heart's True Home* (San Francisco: Harper San Francisco, 1992), 191.

[13] Oswald Chambers, *Prayer: A Holy Occupation* (Grand Rapids, Mich.: Discovery House Publishers, 1992), 8.

[14] E. M. Bounds, *Purpose in Prayer* (1920; reprint, Grand Rapids, Mich.: Baker Book House, 1986), 7–8.

[15] Henry Blackaby, *Experiencing God* (Nashville: Broadman & Holman, 1994), 23.

[16] Bill Hybels, *Too Busy Not to Pray* (Downers Grove, Ill.: InterVarsity Press, 1988), 74.

[17] Henry T. Blackaby and Claude V. King, *Experiencing God* (Nashville: LifeWay Press, 1990), 34.

[18] George Müller, *The Autobiography of George Müller* (Springdale, Penn.: Whitaker House, 1984), 40.

[19] Ibid, 188.

[20] Frank S. Mead, ed., *The Encyclopedia of Religious Quotations* (Westwood, N. J.: Revell, 1965), 344.

[21] Mary Geegh, *God Guides* (Holland, Mich.: Missionary Press, 1991), 2–3.

[22] John Ortberg, *The Life You've Always Wanted* (Grand Rapids, Mich.: Zondervan, 1997), 141.

[23] See <http://www.lifebites.org/archive/archi143.asp>.

[24] John Eldredge, *Waking the Dead: The Glory of a Heart Fully Alive* (Nashville: Thomas Nelson, 2003), 95.

[25] Steve Harper, "The Power of One Life," *Asbury Herald* 113 (Spring/Summer 2003), 5.

[26] A. W. Tozer, *The Pursuit of God* (Camp Hill, Penn.: Christian Publications, Inc., 1993), 82–83.